T0340150

For over thirty years, the Harvard Institutes for Higher Education (HIHE) have been an important resource for the leadership of colleges and universities. HIHE offers world-renowned professional development programs, providing campus leaders with the information and insights necessary for personal and institutional success. All of these programs incorporate the use of case studies. HIHE regularly produces new case studies, to ensure that its teaching materials reflect the most current issues confronting campus leaders. HIHE maintains the country's largest collection of case studies in higher education administration. These case studies are used in professional development programs and in graduate-level courses in educational administration.

To request information on HIHE's professional development programs or to receive a current catalogue of case studies, please contact Harvard Institutes for Higher Education, 14 Story Street, 4th floor, Cambridge, MA 02138

Casebook I

Faculty Employment Policies

James P. Honan and
Cheryl Sternman Rule, Editors

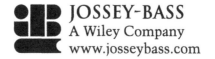

JOSSEY-BASS
A Wiley Company
www.josseybass.com

Published by

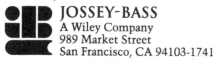

JOSSEY-BASS
A Wiley Company
989 Market Street
San Francisco, CA 94103-1741

www.josseybass.com

Copyright © 2002 by The President and Fellows of Harvard College, Harvard Graduate
School of Education, Longfellow Hall, Appian Way, Cambridge, MA 02138.

Jossey-Bass is a registered trademark of John Wiley & Sons, Inc.

Jossey-Bass books and products are available through most bookstores. To contact
Jossey-Bass directly, call (888) 378-2537, fax to (800) 605-2665, or visit our website at
www.josseybass.com.

Substantial discounts on bulk quantities of Jossey-Bass books are available to corpora-
tions, professional associations, and other organizations. For details and discount information, contact the special sales department at Jossey-Bass.

We at Jossey-Bass strive to use the most environmentally sensitive paper stocks available
to us. Our publications are printed on acid-free recycled stock whenever possible, and our
paper always meets or exceeds minimum GPO and EPA requirements.

Library of Congress Cataloging-in-Publication Data

Honan, James P.
  Casebook I : faculty employment policies / James P. Honan,
Cheryl Sternman Rule.— 1st ed.
      p. cm. — (The Jossey-Bass higher and adult education
series)
Includes bibliographical references (p.   ) and index.
   ISBN 0-7879-5392-X (alk. paper)
  1. College teachers—Tenure—United States—Case studies. 2.
College teaching—United States—Evaluation—Case studies. 3.
College personnel management—United States—Case studies. I.
Title: Casebook one. II. Title: Casebook 1. III. Rule, Cheryl
Sternman. IV. Title. V. Series.
   LB2335.7 .H66 2002
   378.1'22—dc21

2002000608

FIRST EDITION
PB Printing   10 9 8 7 6 5 4 3 2 1

Contents

Preface

The six case studies in this volume focus on various aspects of faculty employment policy. They can be used in a variety of teaching settings, including executive education programs and professional development institutes, graduate courses in higher education administration, and in-service workshops or campus-based planning sessions. Instructors and discussion leaders who are interested in utilizing the cases should consult the companion books, *Using Cases in Higher Education: A Guide for Faculty and Administrators* for general advice concerning the use of case studies as pedagogical tools and *Teaching Notes to Casebook I: Faculty Employment Policies* for specific suggestions and insights regarding possible approaches to teaching each of the cases in this volume.

Each case study in this volume highlights a particular dilemma or challenge regarding faculty employment and is set in an actual institution of higher education. Because these cases were written for teaching purposes, they tend to be longer and broader in scope than traditional "decision cases" with which readers may be familiar. These longer cases not only enable instructors and discussion leaders to address several issues at once, but they also provide readers with sufficient background information and detail to simulate aspects of the actual situations in which the cases' main players found themselves.

Key policy questions on which the cases focus include: Which faculty employment policies enable institutions to recruit and retain the most talented individuals? How is the academy responding to calls for increased accountability among faculty? And, perhaps most important, how can institutions best align faculty employment policies with institutional priorities and departmental needs?

To the greatest extent possible, the cases reflect the full complexity of administrative decision making as viewed through the experiences of academic leaders. As a result, the cases can serve as the basis for sustained and substantive discussions of fundamental policy dilemmas in a number of important areas affecting faculty: tenure policy, the terms and conditions of faculty employment, post-tenure review, non-tenure-track faculty contracts, and the link between faculty employment policies and institutional mission and identity. Thus, issues broadly relating to faculty employment constitute the central theme of the cases in this volume. Subsequent volumes of cases will examine other pressing issues facing college and university administrators, such as planning, curriculum, governance, and budgeting.

Ideally, robust and thorough discussions of these cases can provide insights into how particular policy issues and leadership challenges highlighted in the cases can be translated into one's own experience as an administrator, faculty member, or student of higher education administration.

Following is a brief description of each case in this volume:

Blessed Trinity College*, a small, private college in a large metropolitan area, eliminated traditional tenure in the early 1980s. Efforts to institute long-term faculty contracts and new faculty evaluation procedures stalled for well over a decade. The issue: How can an institution "unstick" itself and make progress in areas that have stymied its leaders for years?

---

*"Blessed Trinity College" is a pseudonym to honor the institution's request for anonymity.

Georgia State University is a public, urban research university that made substantial changes to its faculty policies in such areas as salary inequity, post-tenure review, and part-time employment. The issue: How can an academic administrator effect positive change on several fronts at once while tackling head-on some of the most contentious and complex issues in faculty employment?

Kansas State University is a large, public research institution that faced intervention by its board of regents. The board mandated development of a policy to address chronic low performance by tenured faculty. The issue: How can an institution define and evaluate faculty productivity while taking into account disciplinary distinctions and diverse faculty interests and assignments?

Olivet College, a small, private college, eliminated traditional tenure in the 1970s. Over the past twenty-five years, the college has reconsidered not only its faculty employment policies but its mission and strategic priorities. In addition, Olivet recently considered a return to traditional tenure. The issue: How can a college alter its faculty employment policies during a time of institutional transformation, while simultaneously responding to the distinct needs of multiple campus constituencies?

The *University of Central Arkansas* is a public institution approaching a dramatic transformation on two fronts. First, the institution is offering a pay premium for new faculty who elect non-tenure-track contracts. Second, plans are also under way to potentially revamp the institution into a "charter university." The issues: What is the nature of transformative leadership? and What lessons can be drawn about initiating, managing, and institutionalizing change?

The *University of Minnesota* is a research university that, in the mid-1990s, faced pressure from its board of regents to reexamine the tenure code. The resulting political conflicts made national headlines and wreaked havoc within the university community. The issue: How can an institution respond to external concerns regarding its employment policies while maintaining control of a process with substantive, procedural, and political dimensions?

Each case is accompanied by a list of suggested readings. These citations are designed to help instructors and case users identify pertinent bibliographic resources that provide a broader context for the particular dimension of faculty employment policy examined in each case. In addition, a more general list of selected bibliographic materials dealing not only with faculty issues, but also with organizational change, is included at the end of the case volume. This selection of readings can help instructors and case users to further expand their knowledge of both particular policy issues and relevant research literature and theoretical frameworks.

Acknowledgments

The case studies presented in this volume were developed under the aegis of the Project on Faculty Appointments at the Harvard Graduate School of Education and funded by the Pew Charitable Trusts. We are grateful to Russell Edgerton, the former director of the Education Program at Pew, and to Ellen Wert, a program officer, for their support. Richard Chait, professor of higher education at the Harvard Graduate School of Education and director of the Project on Faculty Appointments, deserves credit and recognition for making this casebook possible in the first place; his intellectual leadership and ongoing encouragement and support provided the impetus and spark for the development of the cases themselves, and for the compilation of the guidebook and teaching notes that accompany this volume. The case authors—Cathy A. Trower, senior researcher; William T. Mallon, then a doctoral student at the Harvard Graduate School of Education (HGSE); and Holly Madsen, a doctoral student at HGSE—were all staff members of the Project on Faculty Appointments. Their excellent work in the development of the cases is much appreciated. We are indebted to Susan B. Kenyon for her editorial leadership throughout the production of this casebook; we could not have done this work without her.

Casebook I

Faculty Employment Policies

1

Blessed Trinity College
Modifying Faculty Evaluation and Contracts

William T. Mallon

On March 11, 1996, Carol Roberts, academic dean and interim vice president at Blessed Trinity College,[1] gathered up several reports from her desk and made her way to a meeting with the college's Contracts and Promotion Committee. As she walked out of her office and down the hall, she reflected, "It seems that one way this institution solves problems is to not finish things. Such an approach asks, 'if no one at the gates is clamoring for a resolution, why solve the problem?'" She quickly reviewed the situation at Blessed Trinity. The board of trustees put a moratorium on tenure in 1980. After the moratorium, new faculty were hired with the understanding that they would have multiyear contracts. Despite repeated attempts to put a faculty evaluation system and multiyear contracts into place, however, neither policy had been implemented. Instead,

William T. Mallon prepared this case under the supervision of James P. Honan, lecturer on education, Harvard Graduate School of Education, as the basis for class discussion rather than to illustrate either effective or ineffective handling of an administrative situation.

This case was prepared for the Project on Faculty Appointments and funded by the Pew Charitable Trusts. © 1998 by the President and Fellows of Harvard College. No part of this publication may be reproduced, stored in a retrieval system, used in a spreadsheet, or transmitted in any form or by any means—electronic, mechanical, photocopying, recording, or otherwise—without the permission of the Project on Faculty Appointments at the Harvard Graduate School of Education.

all faculty hired from 1980 to 1996 had been on a series of one-year contracts.

When she was named academic dean in August 1995, Roberts' charge was to make the multiyear contracts and faculty evaluation system work. She entered the March 1996 Contracts and Promotion Committee meeting with an agenda to make progress on this issue that had stymied Blessed Trinity for over a decade.

Blessed Trinity College

Blessed Trinity College, located in a large metropolitan area, was founded in the 1950s by the Congregation of the Sisters of the Blessed Trinity (CSBT). At that time, the area was experiencing rapid population growth that coincided with increasing demand for higher education for young Catholic women. To fill a niche in that expanding market, the Sisters obtained a charter for a four-year liberal arts college for women. The institution began admitting men in 1972.

In fall 1993, Blessed Trinity expanded to a second campus in a suburban area not too far from the original campus. Through a business-education partnership with a major corporation, Blessed Trinity opened a new facility on the suburban campus in January 1995. As of fall 1996, Blessed Trinity provided liberal arts and professional undergraduate programs and graduate education programs for nearly 3,000 full- and part-time students.

Governance and Policy-Making Traditions

From its beginnings, Blessed Trinity College experienced rapid growth in enrollment, curricular offerings, and academic and administrative staff. One internal document described the college's growth during the first fifteen years as "steady, secure, and even predictable." Despite its growth, Blessed Trinity operated with little administrative infrastructure or formal policy. Long-time faculty report that the college did not have many formal rules or regulations. No faculty search committees existed; rather, the college president interviewed and appointed new faculty members.

In its first several decades, neither the faculty nor the administration of Blessed Trinity focused much attention on promotion and tenure. "In those days," said a senior faculty member, "nobody bothered with a formal process of tenure, though on paper you could have it." Furthermore, he reported, administrators discouraged faculty from applying for tenure. "There was no campus ethos to get it."

Faculty who did apply for promotion and tenure encountered a much simpler course than is typically associated with the tenure process. Describing promotion procedures, the college's 1981 accreditation self-study implied that faculty needed to provide little more than a signed application: "Promotion is not automatic. To initiate this process each fall, four copies of the Application for Faculty Promotion are completed by the eligible candidate. The original copy is retained by the candidate who gives the other three to the Department Chairman. The latter signs the forms, retains one copy, and sends his evaluation and the two remaining copies to the Academic Dean. In turn the Academic Dean recommends the candidate to the President or states his reasons for contrary action. Following review by the Faculty-Administration Committee, the President submits final recommendations to the Board of Trustees."

"There was little evidence needed in one's dossier other than a resume and student evaluations," said John Stephenson, a tenured physics professor who came to Blessed Trinity in 1979. "The real interest was in teaching evaluations and the recommendation from the department chair. Compared to other colleges with which I was familiar, I thought this tenure and promotion process was a piece of cake."

Nor did faculty play a large role in campus governance. A faculty senate established in 1970 included all full-time faculty members. Attendance at faculty senate meetings was mandatory, but enthusiasm for participation was low. One administrator commented, "Faculty back then didn't think too much about the organization and governance of higher education." But the lack of faculty involvement in governance was not solely attributable to lack of interest. Administrators opposed faculty involvement in institutional decision making. The 1981 Accreditation Self-Study, for example, reported that: "[The college must maintain a] balance between the demands of fiscal responsibility, accountability and creative leadership on the one hand and accommodating the expectations of participatory governance on the other. A totally decentralized decision-making structure is not currently viewed as the most effective means of dealing with these new realities."

Many faculty members accepted the administration's powerful role in governing the institution. An economics professor explained, "It was much easier in those days to get decisions made. We would go to the president with our requests and she would say yes or no. That was it."

The Moratorium on Tenure

From 1959 to 1966, tenure at Blessed Trinity was tied to rank; faculty members automatically received tenure after four years as full professors. Then, from the late 1960s to 1980, tenure followed a probationary period of seven years of service without regard to rank. A quota system prevented more than two-thirds of the full-time faculty from receiving tenure. College policy stipulated that, if a tenure opening was not available, tenure-eligible faculty would be offered one-year contracts in the interim.

The board of trustees began to pose questions about the college's faculty appointment policies in the late 1970s. Its concerns centered around three issues: changes in faculty demographics, changing demographics in the religious order, and tenure's effects on the financial well-being of the college.

Changes in Faculty Demographics

Through the 1970s and 1980s, Blessed Trinity experienced constant enrollment growth (see Table 1.1), particularly in professional degree programs such as nursing and education.

Table 1.1. Growth in Full-Time Equivalent Faculty
Members and Students, Fall 1980–1983

	Fall 80	Fall 81	Fall 82	Fall 83
FTE Students	776	878	964	994
FTE Faculty	72	76	97	107

In the 1980s, 75 percent of the college's students and faculty were in the nursing division, and eleven full-time faculty members were added to that department between 1978 and 1983. Many liberal arts departments—biology, chemistry, English, and philosophy—added full-time faculty to provide service courses to nursing students. Business administration also experienced growth: between 1978 and 1983, it added three full-time faculty to its ranks.

Shortly after being named president of Blessed Trinity in 1979, Sr. Mary Johnston realized that many departments had almost reached their tenure quota. This was particularly true of the nursing division. "Because of the strong growth in many departments, we were concerned that a large number of tenure-track faculty would reach the 'up-or-out' decision point and be faced with a quota," Sr. Mary said. "If the department was tenured-in, many instructors would be forced to leave." An internal college document described the problem and advocated eliminating tenure: "Some faculty may be adversely affected if a tenure system is continued at Blessed Trinity College. Within the traditional tenure system, if no tenure slot exists at the college or in a certain division, a faculty member is forced to leave the institution after a probationary period if a quota system exists. This action occurs whether the faculty member is qualified or not. As a result, the tenure decision, if the tenure quota is reached, is based solely on numbers, not on merit."

Changing Demographics in the Religious Order

At one time, Blessed Trinity relied heavily on the religious sisters for faculty positions. In the early years of the college, the percentages of lay and religious faculty were equal. By 1980, however, members of the order filled only thirteen of the forty full-time faculty positions, a trend that continued throughout the decade (see Table 1.2).

The 1981 accreditation team attributed the decline, in part, to changing demographics within the Congregation of Sisters of the Blessed Trinity: "As in the instance of other religious communities, few younger members are entering the order. The median CSBT age—order-wide—is sixty-five. This has implications for the future faculty characteristics and also for long-term financial viability."

The financial benefit that the religious order provided to the college was considerable. The sisters' contributed services[2] represented $375,000 in annual revenue in 1980, 14 percent of the college's revenue from all sources. Administrators and the board recognized the importance of replacing retiring sisters with other members of the religious order, but they could not keep pace with the growing need for faculty.

Moreover, religious faculty did not have tenure, affording the administration a great deal of flexibility. "Tenure was an assured position to lay faculty, but not to religious faculty," explained Professor Stephenson. "Administrators could reassign or remove religious faculty, but they lost that flexibility with lay faculty."

Tenure's Effects on the Financial Well-Being of the College

The impact of tenure on the college's financial condition also concerned the president and the board. "Everything comes back to the

Table 1.2. Changes in Religious/Lay Faculty Composition for Full-Time Faculty, Fall 1980–1989

	F'80	F'81	F'82	F'83	F'84	F'85	F'86	F'87	F'88	F'89
Full-time faculty	40	42	43	46	57	60	60	58	62	66
Full-time religious faculty	13	14	13	13	13	12	10	11	12	13

dollar," Sr. Mary said. She explained the institution's conundrum as follows:

> A tenure system can leave an institution with a large number of high-salaried faculty in departments with low student enrollment. This situation leads to an economic burden on the institution. Additionally, predictions place the modal age of faculty at between fifty-six and sixty-five by the year 2000, with more faculty over sixty-six than under thirty-five. New laws concerning [an end to mandatory] retirement would compound this crisis.
>
> An institution which is heavily tenured also has minimal flexibility. . . . Tenure, in fact, becomes a burden when an institution attempts to adjust its programs and curriculum to meet the educational policies of current and future students. The institution then becomes unable to reallocate resources to best achieve its mission and goals.

Because of these concerns—rapid faculty growth under the constraints of a quota system, fewer religious faculty, and fiscal considerations—the executive committee of the board of trustees suspended the tenure policy at Blessed Trinity College in 1980, grandfathering in faculty members with tenure or on a tenure-track.

Faculty Reaction

Faculty had mixed reactions to the board's suspension of tenure. Several faculty said the announcement came out of the blue because they were not involved in the decision-making process. There was no discussion among faculty about the problem, and "we were given no alternatives," asserted Professor of History William Morrison. "We were under duress to comply, so we voted for something that we didn't want to vote for."

Other faculty reported less concern about the decision. "I don't think faculty felt it was that important when the college did away with tenure," said Professor Stephenson. "There wasn't a strong faculty culture that supported an investment in academic tenure." Another long-time member of the faculty elaborated on the faculty culture: "Colleague relationships among faculty had always been good. There was little concern about tenure because we had a sense of job security. There was a willingness to trade off tenure for another system. Plus, the lack of tenure helps with that environment of collegiality because faculty are not competitive with one another. Faculty colleagues are not willing to sit in judgment of one another. We know each other too well."

Faculty report that there were hostile comments about the decision in private but not in public. "There was remarkable silence from the faculty," said Professor Stephenson. "Many faculty members were accepting of the college's power structure. They didn't demand or expect authority or decision-making power." Another faculty member corroborated this description: "The faculty was docile, waiting for the administration to set the tone. There was a climate of trembling passivity."

The relationship between administration and faculty became more complicated when Sr. Mary hired Richard Stone as academic dean and vice president for academic affairs in 1981. Stone had no higher education teaching experience and was therefore viewed with suspicion by the faculty. "The faculty didn't view the dean as one of their own," recalled one faculty member. "He found it difficult to get respect from department or division heads or from the faculty senate."

The Tenure and Promotion Study Group

Faculty and administrators viewed the suspension of tenure as temporary until the college could decide on a new faculty personnel policy. To that end, in November 1983, Sr. Mary informed the faculty senate of her intention to form a study group to analyze and evaluate the policies of promotion and tenure. The president appointed

Richard Stone as chair of the study group which included six faculty members. Charged with reviewing all aspects of the current tenure and promotion policy and developing a new proposal for tenure and promotion, the group was to present its findings to the president for her consideration.

The study group reported periodically to the faculty senate on its progress. In February 1985, Dean Stone informed the senate that the study group "finds the two concepts [of long-term contracts and tenure] to be very similar." At that point, the study group had not come to any conclusions about recommending either the tenure system or long-term contracts.

The following spring—April 1986—the Tenure and Promotion Study Group presented its final report. It offered five recommendations to the president:

MEMO TO: Sister Mary Johnston, CSBT, Ph.D.
FROM: Tenure and Promotion Study Group
DATE: April 1986
SUBJECT: Study Group Recommendation—
                      Contract System

In response to your charge of April 9, 1984, this study group reviewed the tenure and promotion system at Blessed Trinity College. We have considered all the options of tenure systems and contract systems, applying them to Blessed Trinity in an effort to determine what we believe the most effective resolution for faculty employment status [to be]. We clarified early on in the process that all full-time teaching faculty members presently tenured and those hired in the tenure track system (those hired prior to 1980) remain in the tenure system. Then, as a result of our consideration, we recommend the following for all full-time teaching faculty hired since 1981:

1. All full-time teaching faculty members not in the tenure system be employed according to a contract system. The college contract system will award annual contracts after successful evaluation each year for seven years. After a major evaluation in the seventh year, full-time teaching faculty are eligible for continuing contracts of two to five years, depending on the results of their evaluation and upon the staff needs in their discipline.

2. The President appoint a task force to set up a system of faculty evaluation. This task force will build upon the work of this committee, the work of the Faculty Development Committee, and the academic policies and practices of the office of the Academic Dean in order to recommend a plan for faculty evaluation. This system should be comprehensive, emphasizing (a) annual evaluation of contract faculty, (b) the major evaluation in the seventh year of annual contract, (c) evaluation of continuing contract faculty, related to the years of their contract, and (d) a five year periodic evaluation of tenured faculty.

3. The seventh year evaluation for faculty on annual contracts will be implemented gradually to assure that no faculty member has fewer than three years to prepare for that evaluation. (Faculty may waive this delay and stand for the seventh year evaluation as soon as eligible.)

4. The President designate one faculty committee to review and evaluate faculty qualifications for promotion, tenure, retention of tenure, and major evaluation for seventh year contract candidates. This committee will be chaired by the Academic

Dean, as a voting member, and will have membership from each faculty division. Each faculty division will elect at least one representative from its
full-time faculty. One additional member will be
elected from those faculty divisions whose full-time
faculty exceed 20 percent of the total full-time faculty membership.

5. Every five years the faculty contract system be reviewed and the merits of this contract system relative to the merits of a tenure system be reconsidered.

The faculty approved the recommendations that spring. At the
faculty senate meeting on October 6, 1986, Dean Stone reported
that "the president will consider each of these recommendations for
approval or disapproval, then submit them to the board of trustees
in Spring." In Spring 1987, the board of trustees approved the study
group's recommendations with the following changes: major reviews
for faculty on contracts would take place in the sixth year, not the
seventh; multiple-year contracts would cover two to four years, not
two to five; and a review of the faculty employment system would
occur every ten years rather than every five.

Committees Continue Work on Contracts and Evaluation

In the October 1986 senate meeting, Dean Stone reported that a faculty committee on evaluation would be appointed as recommended
in the study group's report. The committee "would be very small and
fast-acting. It would review, organize, and systematize all the diverse
strands of evaluation which are now in effect and under discussion."
The Faculty Evaluation Committee submitted its final report to Dean
Stone on June 13, 1987. It included recommendations for the
process, timing, and criteria for faculty evaluation in annual reviews,
the major six-year review, and post-tenure review (see Exhibit 1.1 at
the end of this chapter for the proposed guidelines). The committee

recommended (1) the department or division chair conduct annual reviews of all faculty and (2) faculty on multiple-year contracts initiate the review process for the six-year major review, presenting their documentation to the Contracts and Promotion Committee. The Faculty Evaluation Committee did not further elaborate on the process other than to say, "Information will be available through the academic dean's office."

At a faculty senate meeting in spring 1987, Dean Stone reported that the Faculty Evaluation Committee's work "would be finalized in 1987–88 and take effect in 1988–89." Despite the Dean's plan, however, the six-year major review and post-tenure review were never implemented.

The proposed Contracts and Promotion Committee was not put into place until 1989 (see the memo from Dean Stone to full-time faculty in Exhibit 1.2). On November 9, 1989, Dean Stone sent a memo to faculty with a copy of the June 1987 final report of the Faculty Evaluation Committee. The memo stated that the final report "has been approved by the relevant faculty and administrative bodies." He asked faculty, "after you have reviewed the documents, please give your reactions, questions, and suggestions verbally or preferably in writing to my office or me in person." The memo, however, did not indicate when evaluations would be put into place or what steps the dean planned to pursue next.

The Era of "Benign Neglect"

Despite the work of the Faculty Evaluation Committee and the Contracts and Promotion Committee in the late 1980s and the 1990s, Blessed Trinity failed to enact a multiple-year contract system or post-tenure review, even though statements in the faculty handbook implied the system was in place.

Faculty members at Blessed Trinity offered many explanations as to why the system never materialized.

Stability and Security

The administration and faculty had been very stable. From 1981 to 1995, there was no change in the office of the president or vice president for academic affairs. Similarly, there was a perception that little turnover occurred among full-time faculty: from 1980 to 1988, only three faculty members left Blessed Trinity because they were denied tenure or did not receive contract renewal.

Given that stability, "each side was waiting for a shoe to drop," said an economics professor. "Faculty were waiting for the administration to do something; the administration was waiting for the faculty to do something. So, little to nothing happened."

Additionally, job security was not threatened. Blessed Trinity was growing as was demand for faculty. A senior faculty member reported, "There was no en masse resistance or engagement in the problem" from either the faculty or administration. A member of the Contracts and Promotion Committee said, "There was an era of benign neglect here for a long time. The issue just lingered."

Faculty View: The Vice President Contributed to the Problem

Many faculty asserted that Vice President and Dean Stone derailed the progress of contracts and evaluations. Professor Stephenson, who served on the first Contracts and Promotion Committee in 1989, recalled the committee's deliberations about the process and criteria for the six-year major review. (See Exhibit 1.3 for the faculty handbook section on six-year major review.) "Two members of the C and P committee who were nontenurable happened to be at the six-year review point," Stephenson stated. "Both volunteered to be guinea pigs to test the process, but it never happened. It was lost in Richard Stone's office."

Other faculty contended that Stone never acted on a mass of paperwork, reports, and memos. "Every time the C and P committee pushed to implement the process, Stone—who was chair of the committee—didn't call the committee together," declared Professor Stephenson. Additionally, "faculty didn't trust Stone because it was perceived that he routinely withheld information from us," maintained Professor Morrison. "There was a stagnant relationship."

The Vice President's View: A Multifaceted Problem

Stone offered a number of reasons for the lack of implementation while he was in office. First, he claimed that there was a lack of professionalism among C and P committee members. "Faculty often took the stance, 'But we know him and know his work' even if the dossier was incomplete or poorly presented. I had to make guidelines for the dossier review and insist that the committee stick to them. They didn't understand that. They didn't have a real appreciation for governance."

In addition, Stone felt a passive resistance from the faculty as a whole. Sr. Mary noted, "there was not a good relationship between the faculty and the vice president. For example, the faculty wouldn't let Stone be a part of the faculty senate. They didn't see him as one of their own."

Stone also felt a lack of administrative support. "I didn't have any one person to put in charge to make reviews and evaluations happen. I needed a point person, but there was no one in the administration to do it and the division heads weren't trained administrators." At the same time, the college expansion to its suburban location was announced, which "consumed two years of my work. Everything else fell to the side. I wasn't actively pushing for the changes because I was too busy doing other things."

The Issue Arises Again

Because of the faculty's sense of security at the college and the administration's inattention to the matter, the absence of multiyear contracts and faculty evaluation continued for nearly ten years. However, the era of benign neglect ended in 1994. In that year, two full-time untenured nursing faculty members, each with five years of teaching experience at Blessed Trinity, were not renewed because of significant enrollment declines in the nursing division. Changes in the health care industry prompted less need for clinical nurses, and the job market became saturated. Student enrollment in the nursing division dwindled, and Blessed Trinity, for the first time in fifteen years, needed to reduce the size of its full-time faculty. Suddenly, job security at Blessed Trinity became a faculty concern, and the issue of multiyear contracts surfaced once again. "People felt that their job security was threatened, but there were no criteria in place to determine who should stay and who should go," explained Carolyn Lawrence, a junior faculty member. "Faculty feared that the process could be arbitrary."

In addition to the concern about job security, newer faculty began questioning why the six-year review and multiyear contracts hadn't been implemented. Junior faculty member Melinda Gregg said: "When I was offered the job at Blessed Trinity, I wasn't greatly concerned that the college didn't offer tenure, and any anxiety I had was alleviated by the six-year review. It was a good middle ground. I was told that multiyear contracts were in place, and the process was explained on paper in the faculty handbook. It wasn't until after I was here for a year or two that I realized the college only offered one-year contracts, and there were no six-year reviews. The security one expects in academe was just not here. Instead, there was an empty policy."

Newer faculty viewed their needs as different from those of their more experienced colleagues. "Younger faculty had different expectations about teaching, pedagogy, beliefs, and expectations of the working environment," said a junior faculty member. "Senior faculty didn't want to engage in the debate. They had a willingness to accept the administration's proposals because they thought they wouldn't get what they wanted."

Sr. Mary concurred, saying, "faculty became much more aware about their responsibilities to themselves. The quality of the faculty improved and with it the expectations of faculty entitlements."

A Change in Academic Leadership

Carol Roberts became academic dean of Blessed Trinity in August 1995. Prior to this appointment she had held several administrative positions at various colleges in addition to an active teaching career. Stone, who had been academic dean and vice president for academic affairs, remained vice president. Among other responsibilities, Roberts was assigned to work with the Contracts and Promotion Committee to get the process of six-year evaluations moving again. Later that fall, Stone announced his resignation as vice president for academic affairs, and Roberts was named interim vice president. In spring 1996, she was among a number of candidates under consideration for the permanent vice president position.

Faculty were delighted with Roberts' arrival. Various faculty called her "open," "enthusiastic," and "a straight shooter" who listened to faculty, who was interested in faculty views, and who paid attention to their opinions and ideas.

Roberts summarized the environment she found at Blessed Trinity:

> There had not been a lot of thought given to governance. The faculty senate only had two committees: Faculty Welfare and Faculty Development. Other committees were collegewide, which meant they consisted of faculty and administration. Because of the seeming historical mistrust between faculty and administration, faculty didn't view the collegewide committees as representing their interests. Faculty hadn't been given license to do much at all. Faculty perceived that they had a negligible role in governance. As a result, the faculty didn't act at all like faculty are supposed to act. My challenge was to get them to become responsible, and I needed to provide the necessary academic leadership.
>
> Many people transferred their frustration with this faculty evaluation and contracts process onto the former

vice president. I think that was counterproductive. We needed to move on. Before, people weren't ready to move on. By the time I arrived, though, I think the college was poised to move into the mainstream of higher education.

The Contracts and Promotion Committee Meeting: March 11, 1996

In the spring of 1996, Roberts had two goals with regard to promotion and contract policies. First, the committee needed to propose notification dates for nonrenewal of contracts. The faculty handbook included a notification date for first-year faculty members, but there were no dates for faculty who were beyond their first year of employment.[3] Faculty felt vulnerable to potential arbitrary actions by the administration without specific language in the handbook. Second, the committee needed to decide the type, purpose, and goals of extended contracts to propose to the college community. Roberts appointed subcommittees to investigate other colleges' contract systems.

As she waited for the Contracts and Promotion Committee meeting to begin on March 11, 1996, Roberts recalled the disparate voices of the Blessed Trinity community to which she had been listening during the previous year:

A tenured economics professor:
I don't think multiyear contracts are needed. Criteria for evaluation are very vague, and it comes down to a judgment call. We don't have a consensus about what scholarship is, which makes evaluating each other impossible. It is not necessary to subject people to major reviews. My feeling is, if it ain't broke, don't fix it. The less bureaucracy, the better.

A tenured physics professor:
Some younger faculty members feel resentment toward
tenured professors, as if they've been betrayed. They think
we gave it all away. I've had to keep tenure to myself. It
hasn't been something I've been able to rejoice about
because the next person might really resent that I have it
and they don't.

A junior faculty member in humanities:
With no tenure, academic freedom becomes an issue.
You think in the back of your mind before you say anything. People don't want to speak up in the faculty senate. I don't know if there really is an attack on academic
freedom, but it doesn't matter if it's true or not because
faculty have the perception that the administration wants
total control.

A junior faculty member in nursing:
A long-term contract, in my mind, is not the solution. I
want tenure. A multiyear contract won't give us any resolution other than job security, but there still won't be
due process. Now the administration doesn't have to give
any reason for dismissal. We need due process. Tenure
was given up sixteen years ago by a very different faculty.
I think we need it back.

As the C and P committee members gathered around the conference table, Roberts leaned back in her chair and thought, "What
should I do now? What's the best way to make progress in faculty
evaluation and contract policies?"

Endnotes

1. To provide anonymity to the institution, "Blessed Trinity College"
   and names of individuals in this case are pseudonyms. All dates in
   the case have been changed.

2. "Contributed service" refers to the financial benefit the college receives from the sisters' practice of returning their salaries to the institution.

3. The faculty handbook (revised August 1995) stipulated that "dates for notification to those whose contracts will not be renewed are determined as follows: not later than March 1 of the first academic year of service, or at least three months in advance of the termination date of the current contract. An inadvertent failure to meet the deadlines shall not be construed as a renewal of a contract."

Discussion Questions

1. What factors have prevented Blessed Trinity College from implementing its revised faculty evaluation and contract policies?

2. What are the risks and benefits of this lack of implementation for the institution? For the faculty?

3. What should Carol Roberts do regarding the faculty evaluation and contract policies? Why?

Recommended Background Readings

Benjamin, Ernst. (February 1998). "Five Misconceptions about Tenure." *Trusteeship*, 3(1): 16–21.

Bess, James L. (1997). *Contract Systems, Bureaucracies, and Faculty Motivation: The Probable Effects of a No-Tenure Policy*. Paper presented at the Annual Meeting of the American Educational Research Association. Chicago, IL, March 1997.

Byrne, J. Peter. (1997). *Academic Freedom Without Tenure?* AAHE New Pathways Working Paper Series, Inquiry #5. Washington, DC: American Association for Higher Education.

Chait, Richard, and Cathy A. Trower. (1997). *Where Tenure Does Not Reign: Colleges with Contract Systems*. AAHE Working Paper Series, Inquiry #3. Washington, DC: American Association for Higher Education.

Gappa, Judith M. (1996). *Off the Tenure Track: Six Models for Full-Time Nontenurable Appointments*. New Pathways Working Paper Series, Inquiry #10. Washington, DC: American Association for Higher Education.

Licata, Christine M. (June 1998). "Post-Tenure Review: At the Crossroads of Accountability and Opportunity." *AAHE Bulletin*, 3–6.

Mallon, William T. (2000). "Standard Deviations: Faculty Appointment Policies at Institutions Without Tenure." In C. Trower, ed., *Policies on Faculty Appointment: Standard Practices and Unusual Arrangements*. Bolton, MA: Anker .

Miller, Richard I. (1987). *Evaluating Faculty for Promotion and Tenure*. San Francisco: Jossey-Bass.

Exhibit 1.1. Criteria for Faculty Evaluation as Proposed by the Faculty Evaluation Committee, June 1987

Criteria for teaching review:

Course syllabi	Organization of course(s), suitability of assigned coursework to discipline/evaluation procedures, clarity of goals, objectives, [and] grading policies.
Students	Student evaluations, handling of student conflicts or problems, availability for academic consultation with students, evidence of student competencies.
Classroom	Preparation, evidence of expertise, clarity of explanations, poise, classroom atmosphere, student response, use of varying teaching methods, use of supporting materials (such as A-V, handouts), laboratory preparation and supervision (if applicable).
Administrative	Necessary paperwork submitted promptly and efficiently, knowledge and implementation of college policy and procedure.
Other	Use of library (if appropriate), creation of special tools as supplements.

Criteria for service:

Students	Advising, counseling, moderator for club or class, student affairs, all-campus presentation, comprehensive exams, placement activities, availability for student consultation.
Faculty	Faculty senate, faculty institute, senate committees (note: events as listed in Faculty Handbook).

Exhibit 1.1. Criteria for Faculty Evaluation as Proposed by the Faculty Evaluation Committee, June 1987, cont'd.

College	Ad hoc or task-related committees, academic meetings, workshops, alumni activities, recruiting/admissions activities, college events, projects for the college or academic affairs, representing college off-campus.
Community	Civic or cultural groups, parish or city-wide religious activities, volunteer service in the community, civic or community boards, local educational agencies.

Criteria for scholarship:

Professional activities	Membership, attendance at meetings, editorial boards for organization journals, committees or officers in professional organizations.
Presentations	Papers, workshops, talks, panels.
Reviews	Book reviews for publishers, published reviews.
Publications	Books, essays, journal articles, and other educational productions.
Grants	Preparing funding proposals, implementing funded projects, evaluating funded projects.
Development	Preparation of new course(s), cooperative curriculum development or review.
Study	Advanced study, fellowships and awards, workshops, conferences, independent study or coursework in a new or related discipline, professional travel.

Criteria for personal/professionalism:

- Support for the college mission
- Collegiality
- Adherence to Catholic ethical standards
- Serves as professional role model (for students)

Suggested basis for review:

Classroom visit(s); syllabi, tests, and handouts; meetings; consultations (formal and informal); student evaluations; annual report; other reports or documentation; collegial response; student response.

**Exhibit 1.2. Inter-Departmental Memo: Election of Members
of Contracts and Promotion Committee**

DATE:	February 21, 1989
TO:	All Full-Time Faculty
FROM:	Dean Stone

SUBJECT: Election of Members of Contracts and Promotion
Committee

In accord with the report to the President on promotion and
contract, April 1986, we are implementing recommendation 4.

Recommendation 4 (slightly altered):

One faculty committee be designated to review and evaluate
faculty qualifications for promotion, retention of tenure, and major
evaluation for the sixth-year contract candidates. This committee will
be chaired by the Academic Dean, as a voting member, and will have
membership from each faculty division. Each faculty division will elect
at least one representative from its full-time faculty. One additional
member will be elected from those faculty divisions whose full-time
faculty exceeds 20% of the total full-time faculty membership.

I. The *charge* of the Contracts and Promotion Committee is: to
review and evaluate faculty qualifications for promotion,
retention of tenure, and major evaluation for the sixth-year
contract candidates.

II. Liberal Arts is *to elect* two members, Business Administration is to
elect one, and Nursing is to elect two.

III. *Eligibility* to be nominated and elected as a member:

The basic requirement is full-time faculty status for at least five
years at Blessed Trinity College, not counting leaves or sabbaticals. Therefore, those hired by September 198[x] who hold the rank of assistant or
above are eligible. Department chairs, nursing, coordinators, and division
heads are eligible for membership. Their status is full-time faculty.

For the start-up, as a one-time exception only, the division of
Business Administration may elect a faculty member of three years, full-
time faculty status.

Election of Members of Contracts and Promotion Committee
February 21, 1989.

**Exhibit 1.2. Inter-Departmental Memo: Election of Members
of Contracts and Promotion Committee, cont'd.**

IV. *Terms* are normally for two years, with membership terms staggered.

V. The *start-up term* will be as follows so that the membership is
staggered:

Liberal Arts and Nursing:

One member has a three-year term (then new election).
One member has a two-year term (then new election).

Business Administration:

One member for two years (then new election).

VI. Nominations

Liberal Arts and Nursing:

Full-time members of each division are allowed two nominations
of colleagues.

Business Administration:

Full-time members nominate one colleague.
A list of eligible members will be circulated in each division.

VII. Voting

Liberal Arts and Nursing:

All full-time members may vote for two nominees. The two
highest vote getters are elected. The one with the highest number of
votes has a three-year term; the one with the next highest has a two-
year term. If there is a tie, there will be a run-off vote.

Business Administration:

Full-time members vote for one member. The highest vote-getter
wins for the term of two years. If there is a tie, a re-vote will be taken.

VIII. Faculty members on *leave* or *sabbatical* are not eligible to
nominate or to vote or to be elected.

IX. The *next election* will be in the Spring of 1991, wherein three of
the five members are replaced. After that, there is an election
every year to replace the staggered-term members.

Further information will be presented at Division meetings.

Please address questions to the Academic Dean.

Exhibit 1.3. Faculty Handbook Section on Major (Six-Year) Review

4.5.1   *Promotion Review and the Major Review*

4.5.2   *Purpose and Philosophy*

The standards offered here apply to promotion review as well as the major review (the latter also known as the "six-year review.") It is the responsibility of the individual faculty member to initiate the promotion process. That is to say, eligibility dates for promotion of faculty are recorded on the initial faculty member's contract. Accordingly, the faculty member begins the process by adhering to the deadlines and procedures explained in section 4.5.2.

In considering an individual for promotion or for evaluation during the major review, each candidate will be evaluated with respect to his or her proposed rank as well as his or her record of performance in teaching, scholarship, service, and professionalism. Our purpose is to offer a framework of criteria and standards of evaluation within which judgments are made on the present achievements and future potential of the candidate. The major review will take place for all full-time faculty once every six years.

In evaluating the candidate's qualifications within different areas of accomplishment, reasonable flexibility shall be exercised, balancing, where the case requires, heavier assignments and responsibilities in one area against lighter assignments and responsibilities in another. Each candidate is expected to have professional goals which are sound and productive and which can be expected to continue to develop throughout his or her teaching career. In all instances, excellent teaching abilities and intellectual attainment as well as "mission effectiveness" are crucial. Insistence upon these standards for continuing members of the faculty is necessary for the maintenance of Blessed Trinity College's quality as an institution dedicated to the discovery, preservation, and transmission of knowledge as well as the principles of Judeo-Christian values.

2

Georgia State University

Tackling Salary Inequity, Post-Tenure Review, and Part-Time Employment

Cheryl Sternman Rule

The media brims with stories about various evils plaguing higher education. From the high cost of tuition to deadwood senior faculty, from overpaid presidents to overworked junior faculty, from squabbling administrators to governance gridlock, it might appear that academe suffers from chronic disorganization and ineffective policymaking. Enter the College of Arts and Sciences at Georgia State University, which offers a sunny reprieve. There, amid the peach trees and Atlanta skyline, a visionary dean has spent the past eight years tackling head-on some of the most contentious issues in faculty worklife: salary inequity, post-tenure review, and the explosion in part-time instructors to name but a few. And while no approach is flawless, Dean Ahmed Abdelal and his colleagues offer a model of policymaking that not only works but works well. But

Cheryl Sternman Rule prepared this case under the supervision of Richard P. Chait, professor of higher education, and Cathy A. Trower, senior researcher, Harvard Graduate School of Education, as the basis for class discussion rather than to illustrate either effective or ineffective handling of an administrative situation.

does Georgia State University's approach to change and innovation work equally well for everyone? And is this approach one that can be successfully replicated elsewhere?

The University and the College of Arts and Sciences

Located in the heart of downtown Atlanta, Georgia State University (GSU) was founded in 1913 as the Georgia Institute of Technology's "Evening School of Commerce." It has since evolved into a major public research university, with a school of policy studies and colleges of business, education, health and human sciences, law, and arts and sciences. At last count, GSU enrolled more than 30,000 students and employed over 1,400 faculty members in full- and part-time positions.

Along with the College of Business Administration, the College of Arts and Sciences (A&S) was one of the two original colleges of the university. In academic year 1999–2000, A&S offered thirty-four undergraduate majors, twenty-eight master's degrees, and eleven doctoral programs. The college employed 214 tenured faculty, 122 tenure-track faculty, 31 full-time non-tenure-track faculty, 85 full-time visiting faculty, 9 part-time faculty, and 26 part-time visiting faculty. These numbers shifted rather dramatically as the composition of the A&S faculty underwent some major changes in Fall 2000. At that time, there were 387 full-time tenure-line faculty, 47 full-time non-tenure-track faculty, and far fewer than the 85 full-time visiting faculty employed earlier. Many of the once-visiting positions were to convert to regular tenure-track and non-tenure-track lines.

1993. . . A Big Year for Self-Examination

Salary

In 1993, then Associate Dean Abdelal noticed some cases of salary inequity among faculty members in the college. According to David Blumenfeld, associate dean for the humanities and the fine arts,

Abdelal knew from twelve years of experience as chair of biology that practices existed all over the college that were strikingly, if not intentionally, unequal.[1] For example:

- Two distinguished professors were earning $20,000 less than colleagues in the same department with comparable records and equal years in rank.

- A more aggressive chair was able to secure more departmental funding than a less aggressive chair, though their funding applications were equally meritorious.

- Adept negotiators were routinely able to secure higher salaries in the faculty recruitment and hiring process than less adept negotiators, as well as higher yearly raises than merit would suggest.

- A faculty member who happened to publish a book during a year in which new state money was plentiful received a higher raise than a faculty member who published an equally commendable work in a year in which little or no money was available for such rewards.

According to one administrator, "Everyone knew the salaries were out of whack." In the words of another, "Where individual negotiations rather than systematic criteria determine raises, inequities are bound to result." And so they did.

Workload

Salary inequity represented one side of the coin, workload the other. Until 1993, it was nearly impossible to compare faculty members' work across disciplines. For example, an assistant professor of fine arts and an assistant professor of psychology, both with the highest credentials in their fields, operated in wholly different spheres. One taught a small but intense studio art class to majors, the other a mammoth introductory survey course with the help of graduate teaching assistants. Without some way to level the playing field with respect to workload, discussions of salary, raises, merit, and productivity traditionally relied on random criteria at best. "[I]n 1993 the administration of the College of Arts and Sciences at Georgia State University reviewed faculty workloads and concluded that it needed a policy to establish workload comparability across varied disciplines and to provide optimal utilization of faculty talents" (Abdelal and others, 1997, pp. 61–62).

The goal of the new workload policy was to ensure equity while recognizing and supporting faculty members' diverse strengths, talents, and contributions to different areas of the college. (See Exhibit 2.1 for the College of Arts and Sciences faculty workload policy.)

According to Abdelal and others (1997), three main premises undergird the workload policy. First, because the tasks associated with teaching an English course, for example, differed substantially from those involved in overseeing a biology lab, GSU needed "well-defined criteria for comparing workloads across disciplines." The college administration and department chairs worked in concert to create a policy that assigned workload credit to a range of teaching assignments, from conducting ensembles to supervising fieldwork to teaching a large lecture class. This policy, which was approved by the faculty, allotted a faculty member teaching a writing- or technology-intensive course greater "workload credit" than someone teaching an otherwise similar course that was not writing- or technology-intensive. It likewise provided greater workload credit for teaching a large course (with ninety or more students) without a graduate assistant than for teaching a smaller course. The second premise recognized that faculty members at different stages of their careers have different roles and responsibilities. First- and second-year junior faculty, for example, were offered a reduced teaching load so they could concentrate on course preparation and initiating research activities. Similarly, more established tenured faculty were recognized for the greater role they often played in institutional governance. The third premise, and the key to the policy, was that the reward structure needed to recognize comparable effort in diverse arenas.

Post-Tenure Review

Discussions of salary and workload comparability formed a backdrop for the larger issue of faculty productivity in general and tenured faculty productivity in particular. In 1993, three years before the Georgia university system mandated that all institutions conduct some form of post-tenure review, the faculty, administration, and university senate at GSU began discussing the issue on their own. According to Provost Ron Henry, "We were interested in formulating a policy for ourselves before the university system stepped in and imposed one on us."

Those involved in the policy discussions realized quickly that a positive, formative model of post-tenure review, one that identified and rewarded faculty strengths, was more consistent with the concurrent efforts to equalize salaries and workload than the so-called "negative" model of identifying and "punishing" unproductive tenured faculty.[2] (See Exhibit 2.2 for the College of Arts and Sciences faculty post-tenure review policy.)

Phased in over three years, with the first reviews occurring in 1995, the College of Arts and Sciences' post-tenure review policy reflected the college's view that "even the most successful faculty can profit from periodic discussion of their academic endeavors, and that few, if any, faculty, whatever their performance problems, are beyond the hope of real improvement" (Abdelal and others, 1997, p. 65). Along with this positive emphasis, proponents wanted to ensure a smooth review process that minimized the bureaucratic burdens associated with many post-tenure reviews. To that end, reviewers relied on information—including annual reviews, curriculum vitae, teaching evaluations, and publication records—already collected by the dean's office. According to one chair, "The basis for the post-tenure reviews were the annual reviews, which people were doing anyway. So taking five years' worth and combining them was not a major task." In addition, faculty members were asked to write a two-page statement of goals and accomplishments which, according to another chair, "enabled them to be reflective about their work and was a key part of the review process."

Putting It All Together

The discussions about salary, workload, and evaluation could easily have taken place separately, as discrete issues at different times. "But Abdelal's genius," one observer noted, "was in integrating the three initiatives into a cohesive package." In fact, the degree to which each policy informed the other two directly contributed to the success of the policies and to the support each enjoyed among the faculty and administration.

The themes of equity and reward pervaded the three policies, which applied to all ranked, nonvisiting faculty members in A&S (visiting faculty followed separate guidelines). First, the workload policy provided a common yardstick so that faculty could be paid at levels commensurate with their effort and productivity. Then, a merit-based salary initiative kicked in to ensure that "faculty with equal rank and merit in . . . the four discipline areas of the college receive equal compensation." Within each department, an executive committee advised the chair to award each faculty member up to six "points" each for teaching and research and up to four for service; such a quantified approach, when combined with a review of experience, credentials, and annual evaluations, provided a systematic basis for salary increases. In fact, this point system had a built-in checks-and-balances mechanism. Each department chair brought his or her ratings to a meeting with the other department chairs within the same family of disciplines. They then sat down together and, after reviewing all of the performance data, including evidence of teaching effectiveness, either agreed to pass the original chair's recommendation forward to the associate dean or to adjust the rating. This process helped to guard against favoritism; it also held chairs accountable to their peers.

Dean Abdelal explained the impact on salary in detail:

> We . . . approached the question of the relationship between faculty ratings and salaries in two ways. First, we examined the percentage increase in salary over a four-year period. . . . The scattergram and best-fit regression line (see Exhibit 2.3) indicate that higher merit ratings were associated with greater percentage increases in salary. The regression analysis indicates that 57 percent of the variance in percentage salary increase was accounted for by the merit ratings. Specifically, an increase of one point in the merit rating resulted in an additional 5.1 percent being added to the percentage salary increase on average. For example, the average four-year salary increase for a faculty member with a merit rating of 4 (very good) was 15 percent whereas the average four-year salary increase for a faculty member with a merit rating of 5 (excellent) was 20 percent. Second, we examined current salaries. Factors such as rank, time in rank, and area are well known to affect salary and these data are no exception: 77 percent of the variance in salaries was accounted for by these three factors. However, an additional 6 percent of the variance in salaries was accounted for by merit ratings. Specifically, controlling for rank, time in rank, and area, an increase of one point in the merit rating resulted in an additional $4,884 being added to salary on average [Letter dated November 2, 1999, from Dean Abdelal to Richard Chait, professor of higher education, Harvard Graduate School of Education].

One associate professor, who has taught at GSU for thirteen years, appreciated the openness of the system and its reliance on

objective criteria. For him, the availability of the salary data sym-
bolized this openness. "I'm now aware of what people in my department make," he said. "I was clueless for my first six or seven years
here, but now it's open. If there are inequities, they're there for all
to see, and you have an opportunity to discuss them. This process
diffuses suspicion and resentment." Another administrator commented, "There's an audible sigh of relief from junior faculty when
they hear about the rules and the process. They're pleased it's so
open and systematic." A department chair, too, appreciated the per-
vasive candor. "Knowing the process is open forces me to be clear
about the rating I assign and encourages me to really get to know
my faculty."

Like the merit pay initiative, the post-tenure review process
operated according to the principle that merit and positive rein-
forcement must be tightly coupled. According to Associate Provost
Tim Crimmins, the post-tenure review process "has worked very
well in Arts and Sciences because it's tied into the workload model
and compensation system. . . . The anticipation of a reward helps
motivate faculty."

In fact, when the board of regents mandated post-tenure review
for the university system in 1996, the system initially proposed a
stricter, more punitive model. According to Associate Dean Blumenfeld: "In [the proposed] model, only faculty who received consecutive negative annual evaluations would be reviewed, and their
tenure would be in jeopardy if they failed to correct their problems
within three years. At that point, Dean Abdelal argued that although
a negative model may sound tougher and more rigorous, a positive
approach actually gets better results."

And by most accounts, the results have indeed been positive.
For high-achieving faculty, the reviews offered a formalized setting
in which they were praised and given encouragement for continued
excellence. These reviews also directly influenced the merit rating
a tenured faculty member received, which, in turn, influenced his
or her salary and the size of any raise. For those in need of improve-

ment, the review afforded the faculty member an opportunity to devise a plan of action in conjunction with the chair and dean to target areas of weakness and enhance performance. Individual plans varied considerably, but many involved reconfiguring workload, creating a time line by which to complete manuscripts or research experiments, or mentoring by a more experienced colleague. The key to the success of this approach was twofold: the administration was willing to be flexible about work assignments, and, perhaps more significantly, the college was committed to providing the necessary resources to make improved faculty performance a reality.

The Role of Resources

Resources played a key role in both merit-equity and post-tenure review. To advance merit equity, the college undoubtedly needed resources to raise salaries to equitable levels and to offer high performers substantial raises. In the post-tenure review context, these resources, such as graduate research assistants, summer stipends, or release time from teaching responsibilities, formed the backbone of the improvement plans. The ability to award these financial perks may lead one to assume that the College of Arts and Sciences was flush with cash. On the contrary, explained David Blumenfeld, the willingness to allocate resources to these efforts is more a reflection of the college's strategic priorities than of the state filling the college's coffers with gold. In some senses a chicken-and-egg relationship, resources and priorities are mutually reliant. Blumenfeld noted:

> Let me concentrate first on merit equity. Certainly it is true that we had several good years (6 percent raise money in 1996–1999) and that this helped us achieve our objectives more quickly than we otherwise would have. But, in fact, we made progress toward salary equity even in years when state funding was not high. In 1993, for example, when the university received 3 percent for raises, the dean persuaded the chairs that the college

should reserve .5 percent for correcting the most prominent salary inequities. . . . With the chairs' consent, the
dean persisted in holding between .5 percent and 1 percent for merit equity through 1999, by which time the
salary structure in the college was finely tuned. . . [I]t has
now become university policy to provide a fraction of the
salary raises (normally between .25 percent and .75) for
correcting inequities.

Certainly strong state financial support facilitated the college's
ability to meet its goals. Ultimately though, was the college's success
due to increased funding, or rather to its reordering of budgetary priorities? "It was due to both," asserted Blumenfeld, "though reordering
our priorities was the essential factor."

The Dean

When visitors enter Dean Ahmed Abdelal's office, a brass plaque
on his desk stands out: "It's all one budget," it reads. The sign might
as well state, "Special interests and sly negotiators need not apply,
for we're all in this together." And by all accounts, Dean Abdelal
takes this philosophy to heart. In his seven years as dean and his
twenty at the institution, Abdelal has earned the respect of his colleagues and is credited, though perhaps not single-handedly, with
the recent improvements in faculty work life in A&S. According
to one associate professor, "Ahmed's approval rating is over 90 percent. His policies and charisma have driven this success."

After earning his Bachelor of Science degree at Cairo University,
Dean Abdelal completed a Ph.D. in microbiology at the University of California at Davis. He taught in both Cairo and California
before joining the GSU faculty as an associate professor of biology
in 1975. He earned tenure in 1978, and the following year was promoted to full professor and named chair of the biology department.
Dean Abdelal remained chair for thirteen years until, in 1992, he
was named Dean of A&S. Since 1999, Abdelal has also been direc-

tor of the Middle East Center for Peace, Culture, and Development, which, among other initiatives, offers a joint MBA with Cairo University, collaborates in biotechnology research with institutions in Egypt, Israel, and Jordan, and provides advanced pedagogical and English-as-a-Second-Language training for Egyptian teachers. Abdelal has coauthored a textbook for graduate students and produced fifty-five refereed publications.

Dean Abdelal values openness, championing issues he believes in, and works tirelessly to find common ground among squabbling constituents. Dr. Lauren Adamson, associate dean for social and behavioral sciences, commented, "Our dean is indefatigable at building bridges. He will sit down with folks until a bridge is found, or he will go and build it himself."

Dean Abdelal's leadership skills are valued, not only by those who must answer to him, but also by those to whom he himself answers. When the Georgia Board of Regents mandated post-tenure review three years after A&S established its own post-tenure review policy, it ultimately abandoned its preferred model in favor of the one at A&S. In fact, the board was so impressed by the work at GSU, it invited Dean Abdelal and Provost Henry to present their post-tenure review model at a series of workshops for chairs and deans across the state.

Though Abdelal leads by example, his collegial approach relies, by definition, on the strength and commitment of those with whom he works, be they fellow administrators, department chairs, or faculty members. One administrator commented, "There are multiple players in terms of leadership on this campus. The chairs, in particular, have played a major role in all of these initiatives. Chairs here are not just put out on a limb only to be sawed off later." Faculty, too, played a major role in the formation and implementation of the various policy initiatives. Abdelal described the A&S team approach:

> In each case, the dean's office drafted an initial proposal, which it presented to the chairs' council and to the

elected faculty who constitute the College Executive Committee. Discussion in these bodies produced modifications that resulted in proposals with broad-based support in the college. The final proposals balanced faculty prerogatives and administrative concerns and created a system that could be administered equitably and with relative ease. After achieving consensus in the executive committee and chairs' council, the dean presented the workload policy to the full faculty as an initiative that had the support of the college's principal faculty and administrative committees. After we adopted the workload policy, members of elected departmental executive committees assisted in its implementation and helped guide their chairs to administer it in ways designed to further its basic objectives [Abdelal and others, 1997, p. 72].

And while this approach has worked well at GSU, according to one faculty member, "it hasn't worked as well statewide as we would have liked."

What about time? Some would say this is the most precious commodity to overworked faculty members and harried administrators. According to one department chair, "The policies work well, but we had to hold interminable meetings to get where we did. The dean's style is to go over every single nuance."

Part-Time Instructors—the Next Big Hurdle

The time-consuming nature of generating and carrying out the integrated initiatives has not been the administration's only concern. So, too, has the outcome of a recent effort to reduce the number of part-time instructors at the college—a move that struck some as a sincere attempt to promote even greater equity among the faculty and struck others as a weak gesture to placate a discontented, and increasingly vocal, constituency.

The Association of Part-Time Faculty at GSU was founded in the fall of 1998. The group, which initially attracted twelve members, won money and support from the Georgia chapter of the American Association of University Professors (AAUP). Its purpose was to lobby for equitable salary, benefits, office space and equipment, professional development funds, and job security. As on many campuses, part-time instructors (PTIs) at Georgia State had traditionally been underpaid, overworked, and ineligible for many of the benefits and job-related perks that often offset the low salaries faculty members have come to accept as par for their profession. The PTIs' secondary purpose in forming an association was to seek greater respect from their colleagues both in the faculty and in the administration.

According to the *Chronicle of Higher Education,* in the fall of 1998, 189 part-time faculty taught 323 courses at GSU, or "about 36 percent of all the classes offered" (Wilson, 1999, p. A18). Each earned $1,500-$2,000 per course, depending on credentials, and could teach a maximum of eight courses per year. Simple calculations reveal an annual full-time salary of, at most, $16,000, without benefits. At least one part-time instructor took a construction job over the summers to make ends meet.

According to the minutes for the chairs' council meeting on January 6, 1999, Dean Abdelal proposed that: "conversion of PTI positions to faculty appointments with benefits, after graduate students are maximally used, be the budget priority for FY00 for the college. He recommended a salary for visiting lecturers of $24,000 and a workload of eight classes per academic year. He noted that this was 50 percent above the current PTI compensation for teaching, plus roughly 29 percent in benefits, increasing their pay by more than 75 percent. He also said that some of the new positions could eventually be turned into tenure-track positions."[3]

The conversion cost the college $1.7 million the first year, with half of the money coming from the provost's office and the rest from the A&S budget. After passing this proposal through appropriate governance channels, Dean Abdelal announced his plan in April 1999. The original plan was to cut the number of PTI positions in half beginning that fall. In their place, sixty-five new non-tenure-track jobs—ten visiting lecturers (requiring a Ph.D. and paying $30,000 per year) and fifty-five visiting instructors (not requiring a Ph.D. and paying $24,000)–would be created. All of the new positions would be full-time, salaried jobs with full benefits. Current PTIs would be eligible to apply for the new slots.

One might have expected these PTIs to have greeted the news enthusiastically. After all, the salary of a visiting lecturer with a Ph.D., for example, would skyrocket from $16,000 to $30,000 almost overnight. Yet, as one PTI remarked, "We haven't really defined it as a victory. It doesn't answer all the questions, but it is a move in the right direction" (Suggs, 1999, p. 3B).

Among the remaining points of contention were that all of the new positions were "visiting," so there was little job security even for those who had been teaching at GSU for years. Additionally, while the $24,000-$30,000 salary seemed a windfall compared to the old PTI salaries, it still did not compare to the average salary ($36,000-$40,000) of a tenure-track faculty member. Finally, for those faculty members who might have aspired to join the ranks of their tenure-track and, ultimately, tenured colleagues, the heavy teaching load and large classes made devising and carrying out a meaningful research agenda a near impossibility. And according to one faculty member, "It's research and publishing, not teaching, that drives the current tenure-track system."

On the contrary, noted a senior administrator, while many, if not most, research universities place far greater emphasis on research than teaching, "it simply isn't true in our college. Teaching and research are weighted equally in our merit-equity system, and our promotion and tenure manual, which is the authoritative guide for our deliberations, places teaching and research" on par with one another.

Thus while some disagreement over the relative importance of teaching versus research may exist, research, whether of primary, secondary, or equal importance, nonetheless remains an important criterion of advancement in A&S.

The Future

While some dilemmas remain to be resolved, all early signs indicate that the A&S faculty is enjoying a greater degree of collegiality, significantly improved working conditions, and increased opportunities for reward than ever before. If the administration is able to sustain its commitment to improving faculty worklife, Dean Abdelal and his colleagues may well find themselves earning support and admiration far beyond Georgia's borders–perhaps from countless other institutions seeking to create a fairer, more harmonious atmosphere for their faculties as well.

References

Abdelal, Ahmed T., Blumenfeld, David C., Crimmins, Timothy J., and Dressel, Paula L. (1997). "Integrating Accountability Systems and Reward Structures: Workload Policy, Post-Tenure Evaluations, and Salary Compensation." *Metropolitan Universities*, 7(4): 61–73.

Suggs, Ernie. (1999). "Part-Time Faculty Win Raises, May Lose Jobs; Georgia State Cuts to Raise Full-Time Ranks." *Atlanta Journal and Constitution*, May 31, p. 3B.

Wilson, Robin. (1999) "How a University Created 95 Faculty Slots and Scaled Back Its Use of Part-Timers," *Chronicle of Higher Education*, Oct. 22, p. A18.

Endnotes

1. Much of the detail from these policies can be found in Abdelal, A. T., Blumenfeld, D. C., Crimmins, T. J., and Dressel, P. L. (1997). "Integrating Accountability Systems and Reward Structures: Workload Policy, Post-Tenure Evaluations, and Salary Compensation." *Metropolitan Universities*, 7(4): 61–73. Correspondence from Associate Dean David C. Blumenfeld on February 25, 2000, and March 16, 2000, also provided valuable detail.

2. The terms *negative* and *punishing* come directly from interviews with GSU faculty and administration.

3. Excerpt from Chairs' Council Meeting minutes, January 6, 1999.

4. The dean's office in Arts and Sciences includes, in addition to the dean, three associate deans who are responsible for three specific areas; namely, the Social and Behavioral Sciences, the Natural Sciences and Mathematics, and the Humanities and Fine Arts. The office also includes an associate dean for graduate studies and international and community partnerships and an associate dean for undergraduate studies.

Discussion Questions

1. What are the strengths and weaknesses of Dean Abdelal's integrated strategy regarding faculty salaries, workload, and evaluation policies for ranked faculty at GSU?

2. What is your assessment of GSU's conversion of part-time instructors to full-time, non-tenure-track positions? Is this effort good for the institution? For the faculty? Why or why not?

3. What challenges and dilemmas might face GSU regarding faculty employment and worklife in the future? How should Dean Abdelal and his colleagues address them if they arise?

Recommended Background Readings

Abdelal, Ahmed T., David C. Blumenfeld, Timothy J. Crimmins, and Paula L. Dressel, (1997). "Integrating Accountability Systems and Reward Structures: Workload Policy, Post-Tenure Evaluations, and Salary Compensation." *Metropolitan Universities*, 7(4): 61–73.

Diamond, Robert M., and Bronwyn E. Adam, eds. (1993). *Recognizing Faculty Work: Reward Systems for the Year 2000.* San Francisco: Jossey-Bass.

Gappa, Judith M., and David W. Leslie, eds. (1993). *The Invisible Faculty: Improving the Status of Part-Timers in Higher Education.* San Francisco: Jossey-Bass.

Gappa, Judith M., and David W. Leslie. (1997). *Two Faculties or One? The Conundrum of Part-Timers in a Bifurcated Workforce.* New Pathways Working Paper Series, Inquiry #6. Washington, DC: American Association for Higher Education.

Hansen, W. L. (1988). "Merit Pay in Higher Education." In David W. Breneman and Ted I. K. Youn, eds., *Academic Labor Markets and Careers* (pp. 114–137). New York: Falmer Press.

Layzell, Daniel T. (1999). "Higher Education's Changing Environment: Faculty Productivity and the Reward Structure." In William G. Tierney, ed., *Faculty Productivity: Facts, Fictions, and Issues*. New York: Falmer Press.

Licata, Christine M., and Joseph C. Morreale. (1997). *Post-Tenure Review: Policies, Practices, Precautions*. New Pathways Working Paper Series, Inquiry #12. Washington, DC: American Association for Higher Education.

Reichard, Gary W. (1998). "Part-Time Faculty in Research Universities: Problems and Prospects." *Academe*, 84 (January/February): 4–43.

Rhoades, Gary. (1996). "Reorganizing the Faculty Workforce for Flexibility." *Journal of Higher Education*, 67(6): 626–659.

Exhibit 2.1. Georgia State University, College of Arts and Sciences, Faculty Workload

Contents:

Teaching Load Expectations

Course Releases

1. Laboratory or studio courses

2. Dissertations, theses, etc.

3. Time purchase

4. Research/creative activity

5. Major service roles

6. New tenure-track assistant professors

7. Other releases

Teaching Load Expectations

The normal workload includes teaching, research/creative activity, and service activities. Within this normal workload, the teaching load is five courses or equivalent per academic year. It is the goal of the College to consider a four-course teaching load, when sufficient resources become available. Faculty members who are not carrying out significant research/ creative activity over several years and/or significant service activities are

Exhibit 2.1. Georgia State University, College of Arts and Sciences, Faculty Workload, cont'd.

expected to dedicate the balance of their workload to instruction. The extent of this higher level is to be determined by the Chair/Director, and the extent should relate directly to the amount of research and time-consuming service the faculty member is engaged in. Faculty members who are not engaged in research or service are expected to teach nine sections per year. The annual raises for faculty who are assigned a teaching load higher than five courses or the equivalent per academic year will be based on their performance in the area(s) identified by their workload assignment.

Each department will develop a plan to maintain its current enrollment level after conversion to the Semester System. Departmental plans may include relying on factors such as increasing class limits, use of non-tenure track, Graduate Teaching Assistants, and Part-time Instructors to maintain enrollment levels.

Course Releases

A reduction in the teaching load of an individual faculty member is determined by the Chair/Director in consultation with the Dean's Office. A number of reasons are recognized as justification for a reduction in teaching load. The following considerations can be used for justification of a teaching load of less than five courses or equivalent per academic year:

1. Laboratory or studio courses

In general, the contact hours rather than the credit hours should be considered in laboratory, studio or other similar courses. The extent of this consideration is determined by the Chair/Director in coordination with the Dean's Office.

2. Dissertations, Master theses, Honors theses, practica, large sections, writing intensive courses, technology-enhanced courses and independent studies

Equivalent workload in these areas will be determined by each Chair/Director in coordination with the Dean's Office.

**Exhibit 2.1. Georgia State University, College of Arts
and Sciences, Faculty Workload, cont'd.**

3. Time purchase

The percent salary needed will be negotiated with the chair on the basis
of the specific workload profile for the faculty member. However, the
percent salary cannot be less than 1/9 of the faculty member's salary for
each course release. The timing of the release semester must be negotiated with the Chair/Director.

4. Research/creative activity

In coordination with the Dean's Office, each Chair/Director can determine
in advance an annual number of course releases for research/creative
activity. These course releases are determined by the Chair/Director to
faculty members in order to enhance faculty research productivity, thus
strengthening department/school research/creative programs. Faculty
members who have received a course release should demonstrate productivity in order to be eligible to receive additional releases.

5. Major service roles

Major leadership roles in the College or the University will be considered
as part of the faculty workload. Examples of these are service on the College Executive Committee or University Senate Executive Committee,
chair or subcommittee chair of University Senate committees, membership on the College P & T committee, departmental graduate or undergraduate directorships, and service to the profession on a national level.

6. New tenure-track assistant professors

The normal teaching load for this group of faculty will be four courses
per academic year for the first three years to provide more adequate
opportunity for scholarship and course preparation.

7. Other releases

In addition to these justifications for reduced teaching load, the Chair/
Director may provide other justifications contingent on approval of
the Dean.

Exhibit 2.2. Post-Tenure Review Policy

The University Policy of Promotion, Tenure, and Development for Tenure Track Faculty mandates a cumulative review of tenured faculty members every five years. This policy states that post-tenure review should provide "an opportunity to assess faculty development goals and achievements" and "assistance to faculty in ensuring continuous intellectual and professional growth."

The University Policy provides a general structure for post-tenure reviews; each unit specifies its own guidelines. This document outlines the guidelines for the College of Arts and Sciences. The overarching aim in the College is to employ a formative process that will connect the review of prior work with on-going discussion of a faculty member's goal setting, development, and workload profile.

According to University policy, the review must be conducted by an elected committee. In the College, these reviews will be conducted by the three Area Committees on Promotion and Tenure. One Area Committee represents humanities and the fine arts, one mathematics and the natural sciences, and one the social sciences. As specified in the College Bylaws (revision of May 18, 1994), each standing committee is composed of faculty members elected by the area of the College it represents.

Post-tenure reviews will address accomplishments in teaching, advising and serving students, in research/scholarly/creative activity, and in service. According to University policy, the review will be based on available information from the last five years. In the College of Arts and Sciences, these materials will include annual reports, curriculum vitae, publications/creative achievements, and evidence of teaching effectiveness. Faculty will also provide a 2 to 3 page statement that provides contextual information about accomplishments during the past five years as well as career goals and plans.

The review process, instituted in Spring 1995, begins five years after a faculty member's most recent promotion and continues at five year intervals unless interrupted by a further promotion or impending candidacy for promotion within a year. Faculty who formally notify the Dean's Office of their plans to retire prior to January of their review year are exempt from review. Similarly, faculty members who notify their chair of their interest

Exhibit 2.2. Post-Tenure Review Policy, cont'd.

in being considered for promotion in the academic year of their review will be exempted.

For each faculty member undergoing review, the chair will provide his/her assessment of effectiveness in teaching, research, and service and the chair's perspective on the faculty member's written statement. The chair will also provide the committee with an updated vita, copies of the past five annual reports, and available documentation related to teaching and professional achievements for the past five years. The Committee will provide a written report of its review to the Dean's Office by the end of April. After adding a one-page letter of analysis, the Dean will forward all materials to the Provost. In accordance with University guidelines, faculty will receive from the Dean's Office a copy of the entire review once it is completed.

After completion of all assessments, a conference will be held between the Dean, the appropriate associate dean, the chair, and the faculty member. This conference will produce a plan focusing on professional goals and/or workload profile, for subsequent approval by the Dean. The Dean, in consultation with the chair, will be responsible for monitoring progress through the regular process of annual faculty evaluations.

Exhibit 2.3 Percentage Increase in Salary over Four Years

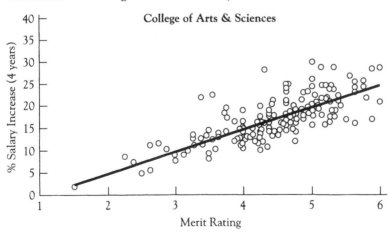

3

Kansas State University

Evaluating and Addressing Chronic Low Achievement

Holly Madsen

W hen Provost James Coffman received a list of seven recommendations regarding faculty evaluation from the Kansas Board of Regents in March 1995, the message was clear: "The board expects [the recommendations] to be implemented in this important area of accountability to our public" (see Exhibit 3.1 at the end of the chapter). The sensitive issues addressed in the memo grew, in part, out of the board's reaction to public complaints about higher education generally, and a rising clamor over faculty accountability more particularly. As John Welsh, Executive Director of the Board of Regents, explained, "Over the years, some faculty members have been dismissed over low performance, and the regents saw these cases drag out over time in the media. They wanted to empower K-State and the other university administrators to do something about it."

Holly Madsen prepared this case under the supervision of Richard P. Chait, professor of higher education, Harvard Graduate School of Education, as the basis for class discussion rather than to illustrate either effective or ineffective handling of an administrative situation.

This case was prepared for the Project on Faculty Appointments and funded by the Pew Charitable Trusts. © 1998 by the President and Fellows of Harvard College. No part of this publication may be reproduced, stored in a retrieval system, used in a spreadsheet, or transmitted in any form or by any means—electronic, mechanical, photocopying, recording, or otherwise—without the permission of the Project on Faculty Appointments at the Harvard Graduate School of Education.

The head of the Department of Philosophy, James Hamilton, said, "The regents were reacting to the legislature, which gets phone calls from parents. They are reacting to the broad perception that professors don't work very hard."

The recommendations called for regular evaluations of faculty members by multiple parties, specifying that the university should use "instruments to measure student rating of instruction [that] solicit, at a minimum, student perspectives on (a) the delivery of instruction; (b) the assessment of learning; (c) the availability of the faculty members to students; and (d) whether the goals and objectives of the course were met." The board also directed the university to develop a goal-setting process and regularly engage department heads in the evaluation of individuals.

In addition, the regents directed department chairs to clearly "allocate the amount of effort the faculty member will devote to teaching, research, and service" based on institutional and departmental goals. The board noted, "merit evaluation of faculty should follow this agreement." Most contentious among the regents' recommendations was the call for a new policy on "chronic low performance." Section 7a of Exhibit 3.1 reads: "Each campus should i) provide assistance for faculty renewal and development, ii) define chronic low performance, and iii) examine dismissal policies to include chronic low performance, *despite all assistance*, as an indicator of incompetence."

It was the latter recommendation, in particular, that set in motion a process of spirited negotiations between and among faculty leaders and administrators culminating in a new university policy intended to identify and address "chronic low achievement."

Kansas State University

Set in the rolling Flint Hills of northeast Kansas, Kansas State University sprawls over a 664-acre campus in the town of Manhattan, 125 miles west of Kansas City. Known as K-State, the university was founded in 1863 as a land-grant institution under the Morrill Act. In 1997–98, K-State enrolled 20,300 students and employed 1,600 faculty members (including graduate assistants), of whom 900 were tenured. In recent years, the university has placed particular emphasis on the synthesis of scholarship and teaching. In 1997, K-State was one of ten research institutions in the nation to receive a National Science Foundation award recognizing its work in integrating research and education in the sciences.

The Kansas Board of Regents is a nine-member body that oversees K-State and five other state universities, including the University of Kansas. Members are appointed by the governor and confirmed by the Kansas Senate.

Creating a Context for Collaboration

On a humid spring day in his office in Anderson Hall, Dr. Coffman, who had been provost for eleven years, reflected on the series of events spurred by the regents' mandate.

From the outset of his term as provost, Coffman set the tone for collaborative and cooperative work with the faculty—an approach followed at K-State since the beginning of President Jon Wefald's administration in 1986. "The process was advanced a few years ago, in some ways, when the vice president for administration and finance, the legislative liaison, and I visited every college of the university to discuss the legislative budget for the university," Coffman recalled. State funds for higher education were not plentiful, and he considered it important to discuss the matter with deans and department heads. At about the same time, Coffman began inviting the leadership of the faculty senate to the national "Faculty Roles and Rewards" meetings of the American Association of Higher Education. By encouraging participation in each of these settings, the provost helped set the stage for productive discussions between the administration and the faculty on issues critical to the life of the university.

According to Coffman, it was also important to the process that the university had spent several years on its own adjusting the annual evaluation process before the regents' call for new policies and practices for faculty performance reviews. In 1991, the board of regents established a task force for improving faculty evaluation, bringing together a broad-based group that included one member of the board, two chief academic officers from the Kansas system, two faculty members, two students, and two members of the regents' professional staff. The group produced a general statement on faculty evaluation in 1992. During the years 1990 through 1993, K-State revised its promotion and tenure policies, overlapping with the board of regents' task force efforts. While each department developed its own standards and criteria, each college established an advisory committee to evaluate these standards and criteria. In addition, the college advisory committees were charged with reviewing candidates for promotion and tenure and with making recommendations to their deans for each candidate. Provost Coffman believes the collaborative environment that the board, faculty, and administration cultivated over these years was essential to developing the new policy.

John Heibert, a cardiologist and new chair of the Kansas Board of Regents, visited K-State around the same time as the board's list of recommendations for greater accountability arrived on campus. As an adjunct clinical professor at the University of Kansas, he was perhaps better positioned to make the regents' case than the previous chair who was a banker and a businessman. Former faculty senate president and dean of the College of Technology and Aviation at K-State's Salina Campus, Dennis Kuhlman, recalled that during his visit, Heibert reiterated the regents' conviction that some level "of 'deadwood' [existed] throughout the university system."

The provost's first step after release of the recommendations was to give the faculty senate a chance to address the board's concerns. Stepping to one side, he asked faculty leaders to guide the effort. He recalled, "I said, 'What is the faculty going to do about this?' The senate president replied, 'We'll step up to the plate.'" One policy objective, as the provost described it, would be to "nudge the driftwood into action," while another would be to establish a means for reallocating effort among faculty members.

From the outset, Provost Coffman paid close attention to the political aspects of the process. The president and provost met with the leadership of the faculty senate every month. He said another crucial element was that KSU "had three [consecutive] senate presidents who believed in this evaluation process." Coffman noted, "You can't just say 'here's the plan.' It takes time. You have to wade into the thicket, get faculty to buy in, then work through the decision-making process." He added that the significant tenure of K-State administrators was also valuable: "If I had only been here three to five years, this would never have been accomplished."

The Chronic Low Achievers Task Force

In fall 1995, then-Faculty Senate President Kuhlman formed a special task force to address the call for a new policy. The task force of seven included primarily faculty members, as well as department heads, and one dean. The group was charged with reviewing existing policies and procedures to ensure that: (a) assistance is provided for faculty renewal and development; (b) an adequate definition of chronic low performance is included in evaluation, promotion, and tenure criteria guidelines; and (c) dismissal policies include provisions for including chronic low performance as an indicator of incompetence.

To this point, discussions about the regents' resolution and chronic low achievement policies had not been especially heated. However, many faculty leaders raised a furor when the regents suggested that chronic low achievers could be identified from a list of faculty who had repeatedly received low salary increases. In view of the fact that the university had lacked the funds to offer significant salary increases in recent years, many faculty members viewed this proposal as flawed and unfair. According to Kuhlman, the regents wanted to label "anyone who had less than a 1 percent raise as dead-wood." He said, "We refuted that by reminding them that all university raises had been small in the first place, and for that reason it was possible for a productive faculty member to receive a small raise." A member of the Faculty Affairs Committee, Associate Professor of Agronomy Gary Pierzynski, described the regents' proposal as a turning point for faculty leaders. It was clear that "if *we* didn't do something, the regents would do something to us."

Pierzynski, chair of the Chronic Low Achievers Task Force, said, "We began by examining the regents' memo and decided that we wanted to avoid a full-blown post-tenure review policy," which he described as a repeated retenuring process that would force tenured faculty members to continually reapply for their jobs. While recognizing that the university needed to respond to the concerns expressed by the board of regents, the committee wanted to find a middle ground, stopping short of extreme measures that might change the nature of faculty appointments or the faculty culture at K-State.

The task force went to work, conducting a wide-ranging review of existing faculty evaluation policies in departments and colleges across the university. The group then drafted a policy statement on chronic low achievement intended to put pressure on department heads to conduct more systematic annual evaluations and to document them in a substantive manner that would serve multiple purposes. By August 1995, the Chronic Low Achievers Task Force asked the Faculty Affairs Committee to consider the newly drafted language on chronic low achievers as a proposed addition to the faculty handbook.

Negotiating New Measures

In meetings of the Faculty Affairs Committee and the full faculty senate, the strongest opponents to the notion of a policy to address low faculty performance argued that it was an infringement on the rights earned by tenured faculty members. Kuhlman recalled that some faculty protested ardently on the grounds that "any comprehensive evaluation after the tenuring process is tantamount to revoking tenure." Physics Department Head James Legg said he and others were vehemently opposed "because of what it does to faculty morale. It sends the wrong message."

At the other end of the spectrum, a faculty senator who helped shepherd the new policy through the approval channels described the resistors as a particularly cynical lot that "went as far as to say 'This will be the death of tenure.'" Likewise, David Balk, another former senate president, now head of the Department of Family Relations and Child Development at Oklahoma State University, argued that, contrary to the views of some dissidents, "tenure is not an entitlement to be nonproductive. Tenure protects academic freedom, but we cannot hide behind tenure to cover low productivity."

Still other faculty leaders pointed out that the university already employed multiple layers of evaluation. The minutes of the December 12, 1995, faculty senate meeting state: "Senator Michie believes the Faculty Handbook and the AAUP Guidelines provide sufficient protection for the university in cases of low achievement by tenured faculty. She suggested we should simply tell the Regents that 'We're already covered.'" As Physics Department Head James Legg put it, "Our faculty are already evaluated so thoroughly, there's no place to hide."

Some faculty believed the real problem was "public relations and public image," namely, misperceptions among the public and the legislature about what faculty members do. Former Senate President Balk commented, "Most people don't understand what faculty do. We haven't done a good job of telling them." In addition, Kuhlman noted, "There's a nationwide misperception that there's a lot of deadwood on the faculty."

Others were particularly offended by the suggestion that there are large numbers of unproductive faculty members at K-State. Pierzynski argued that the situation, in fact, was just the opposite:

"I work in a department of chronic overachievers—highly competitive and productive." To this point, Kuhlman added that the term "average" becomes "extremely difficult to define. Faculty who find themselves in a small department surrounded with overachievers are severely penalized by an emphasis on merit."

Shared Governance in Action: Enacting a New Policy

After months of spirited discussion, debate, and negotiation, the language drafted by the task force moved through the Faculty Affairs Committee (responsible for formulating policies on matters such as faculty employment, tenure, promotions, and workload). The minutes of the faculty senate meeting in December 1995 record that "Senator Pierzynski moved to approve new faculty handbook section C31.5. An amended version of the policy passed with a vote of 45 'yes' and 23 'no.'"

How was the faculty senate ultimately able to pass a "chronic low achievers policy?" The provost attributed the policy's passage to close collaboration between the administration and the faculty. Professor Kuhlman echoed this view, stating, "K-State has a shared governance system that operates at a high level. It works as a result of open communication." In a similar vein, the regents praised the "sincere cooperation of the faculty senate presidents," and a senate president, in turn, complimented the regents, describing them as "intelligent participants."

However, not everyone painted such a rosy picture. Philosophy Department Head Hamilton, who counted himself among the strong opponents to the new policy, described the situation as more divisive: "My colleagues work very hard, yet the regents are telling us 'We don't care what you say, we want to find out who's not doing anything.' We were simply told to create a policy, irrespective of the real situation at hand." Hamilton pointed out that the faculty senate is comprised of approximately two-thirds faculty and one-third staff and administrators, and that when it came to a vote, about one-half of the faculty members who served on the senate voted against C31.5. Another department head remarked that he and his colleagues were "burned and embittered by the whole thing."

Still others attributed passage of the policy to political realities. That is, the issue was not whether there would be a policy, but rather who would write it. Drafting the policy in the senate was a means of taking the matter into "our own hands rather than allowing something to be done to us." If the faculty had not addressed the board's concerns, it is very likely that the regents would have proceeded anyway, and perhaps even have adopted a comprehensive post-tenure review policy. "We didn't need C31.5 to say that incompetence is unacceptable," Professor Legg commented. "We needed it because the regents felt that they needed it from every university in the system, to show the legislature that we're not sheltering unproductive faculty with tenure." At the December 12, 1995, faculty senate meeting Senate President Kuhlman explained that "the BOR staff and some members had reviewed our faculty handbook. They did not think our [policy on] 'incompetence' covered 'chronic low achievers.' We needed something to satisfy the regents and the public."

A statement on chronic low achievement was, in the minds of many, a lesser evil than a board-crafted policy on chronic low achievement or worse, a full-scale post-tenure review system. From that perspective, observed a former senate president, the new policy was "a means to safeguard tenure." Moreover, he commented, in order to sell the policy, "we pointed out that we believed there would be very few professors who [would] fall into that [below-minimum-standards] category." Whatever the mix of motives and rationales, a new policy was enacted.

The Result

C31.5. *Chronic Low Achievement.* Chronic failure of a tenured faculty member to perform his or her professional duties, as defined in the respective unit, shall constitute evidence of "professional incompetence" and warrant consideration for "dismissal for cause" under existing university policies. Each department or unit shall develop a set of guidelines describing the minimum acceptable level of productivity for all applicable areas of responsibility for the faculty, as well as procedures to handle such cases. In keeping with regular procedures in matters of tenure (C112.1 and C112.2), eligible departmental faculty will have input into any decision on individual cases unless the faculty member requests otherwise. When a tenured faculty member's overall performance falls below the minimum acceptable level, as indicated by the annual evaluation, the department or unit head shall indicate so in writing to the faculty member. The department head will also indicate, in writing, a suggested course of action to improve the performance of the faculty member. In subsequent annual evaluations, the faculty member will report on activities aimed at improving performance and any evidence of improvement. The names of faculty members who fail to meet minimum standards for the year following the department head's suggested course of action will be forwarded to the appropriate dean. If the faculty member has two successive evaluations or a total of three evaluations in any five-year period in which minimum standards are not met, then "dismissal for cause" will be considered at the discretion of the appropriate dean [Excerpted from the Kansas State University Faculty Handbook, Section C: Faculty Identity, Employment, and Tenure].

Local Autonomy for Academic Departments

A critical element of the new policy was delegation of defining the guidelines for determining a "minimum acceptable level of productivity. . .as well as procedures to handle such cases" to individual academic departments. The faculty members of each department, working as a group, were to devise standards and evaluation criteria for minimum acceptable performance. Department heads were given the responsibility to identify the point at which this threshold had been crossed, to set in motion remediation activities to address the situation, and if necessary, to determine the point at which dismissal for cause might be considered. The policy was structured so that in a case where Section C31.5 was triggered, the faculty member in question would be given at least one year, and potentially as many as four years, to improve his or her performance before dismissal for cause could be considered.

By early 1997, department heads and faculty members began adapting their performance evaluation practices to comply with Section C31.5. While Provost Coffman described this provision as "fundamental to implementation of C31.5," he also stated "this will vary, consistent with departments' evaluation systems. Consequently, there will be many approaches that will accomplish this task. . . . Some departments have adopted a quantitative approach, while others have chosen a more qualitative approach. Neither method will be rejected on that basis alone" (Letter to Deans on March 12, 1997). Of greater concern to the provost was that the policies be clear, even-handed, and consistent with the university's performance expectations of faculty.

The faculty made a conscious decision to have departments develop their own standards because, as Pierzynski noted, "they know their disciplines best." John Havlin, former faculty senate president, described this provision as a key component of the new policy and one that enabled C31.5 to gain approval. However, in the faculty senate meeting of June 11, 1997, Senator Aruna Michie pointed out that "individuals and departments are not totally free to set standards, since departmental standards, at least, must be approved by the deans and the provost." The possibility of uniform, university-wide standards was raised but deemed infeasible in the same meeting because "K-State's departments and colleges had very different missions, and therefore very different job descriptions."

Balk remarked, "The provost and the deans will help make the differences between departments equitable." However, the potential for taking advantage of the department's prerogative cropped up early in the process of developing guidelines, when Balk observed that "in some departments there was an effort to make expectations so low that no one could fail them." Noting the disparities between departmental standards, some faculty members began to wonder whether the system could work fairly.

In 1997–1998, each department drafted guidelines for minimum acceptable levels of productivity and submitted them to the provost's office for initial review by Jane Rowlett, Director of Unclassified Affairs and University Compliance. In the first round, Coffman and Rowlett returned draft guidelines to nearly two-thirds of the departments for additional work. According to Coffman, most of the unacceptable drafts were returned because they failed to adequately address the question of "what to do when a faculty member is failing or fallow in one major area [but not in other areas]." Other drafts failed to describe the department's means of triggering the C31.5 process.

Some departments defined minimum standards in a very broad way, while others enumerated tasks and set acceptable percentages of completion. Table 3.1 at the end of this chapter outlines policy proposals from three departments. The guidelines for one natural science department were very specific and rigorous, while a social science department's minimum standards were vague and skeletal. Between these extremes, a department in agriculture used an evaluation process whereby "the head rates faculty on each applicable criterion (examples include teaching improvement, research focus and aggressiveness, and peer evaluations) and develops an overall rating in each of the following categories: teaching, research, extension, nondirected service, and directed service activities." The final merit score was weighted according to the percentage of effort devoted to each area. An overall rating of less than 60 on a 100-point scale in any of the four categories would indicate failure to achieve the minimum acceptable level of productivity.

There was no clear consensus on whether any one approach to defining minimum standards would be most effective. Rowlett pointed out that while the evaluation procedures that relied heavily on a formula to identify productivity levels appeared to be very thorough, some faculty and administrators worried that this method might dampen creativity or discourage interdisciplinary scholarship and teaching. Concern was especially high where the criteria explicitly rewarded scholarly publications only in certain disciplinary journals.

Interpreting "Scripture"

Rather than marking the end of a successful round of policymaking, the passage of Section C31.5, in fact, opened a new series of discussions about the point at which the policy would be invoked. On January 8, 1996, Coffman wrote a memo to the university's deans describing how the new faculty evaluation process should be implemented:

> Department Heads are to meet individually with each faculty member. . .for the purpose of establishing, in general terms, the distribution of the faculty member's time and effort for the coming year, and what the expectations should reasonably be as to performance standards and criteria. The results of this discussion should be specific and unique for the individual, and consistent with more general criteria and standards which should exist in each department's document on criteria and standards for evaluation, promotion, and tenure. Any problem areas which exist from the previous year(s) should also be clarified, along with a plan for addressing them.
>
> At the conclusion of the year, the annual merit evaluation is to include, along with whatever other numerical

ratings and narrative, an overall assessment of "meets expectations, exceeds expectations, or fails to meet expectations". Thus, we will cease to compare faculty with each other, and instead compare performance with individualized expectations. . .Salary adjustment is then reconciled with each of these groups, with the general assumption that "fails to meet expectations" will result in no salary increase.

During this period, the provost met frequently with the Council of Deans, department heads, and faculty leaders, including the Faculty Affairs Committee. In February 1996 he presented a series of workshops for deans, associate deans, and department heads on faculty evaluation as related to the new policy on chronic low achievement. While Coffman was pleased with the "level of ideas and interaction that took place" in the workshops, he also recognized the need to clarify the definition of what would constitute an overall rating of "below expectations."

In Coffman's view, the assignment of responsibilities and setting of goals for each faculty member was primarily a resource allocation process. With this in mind, on February 22, 1996, he wrote to deans and department heads, stating: "In instances where one or *more critical*, or *essential*, areas of an individual's work (consistent with the department's document on criteria and standards) are found to fall below expectations, the *overall* [emphasis added] evaluation should be considered to fall below expectations. This means that if a person is consistently falling below expectations in a critical area of work, by definition we are wasting the resources attached to that activity." The provost explained further that if this situation occurred, Section C31.5 would trigger "a serious assessment of the individual's role in the department, as well as the establishment of a meaningful remediation development plan."

Coffman's interpretation was highly controversial. The contention that, if a small percentage of a faculty member's appointment—for instance, a 20 percent assignment to research—was deemed substandard, the entire evaluation would be considered substandard, "evoked a real firestorm," according to Balk. Professor Legg voiced the fear among some faculty members that a department might "force a small percentage of responsibility in an area that the faculty member cannot meet." The faculty senate meeting minutes for April 9, 1996, reported:

Faculty Affairs met just prior to the Senate meeting with Provost Coffman to discuss section C31.5 of the Faculty Handbook, as requested by the Senate. Specific questions regarded the Provost's call for individualized faculty evaluations, under which a faculty member not meeting his/her expectations would not be given a raise, even though s/he meets minimum department standards. In addition, he specified that "chronic low achievement" referred to failure to meet one or more standards deemed "critical" in the department's mission statement. Senators expressed concern about the seeming variance from the Senate's specification for "overall" performance. Senator Robert Poresky voiced his concern about a faculty member with a 10 percent service "goal" and no time to fulfill it, in which case a strict reading of "overall" would mean that the entire evaluation, however excellent the other components, would be below minimum standards.

For some faculty, the discussion took on the tenor of a turf battle, and the provost's interpretation of the new policy was viewed as aggressive interference. In the April faculty senate meeting, Pierzynski said Provost Coffman had "'drawn a line in the sand' with the strict reading of the term 'overall'" and reiterated Senator Jennifer Kassebaum's suggestion after the last senate meeting that "perhaps the provost might like to only 'recommend' that interpretation."

In an attempt to clarify these issues from the faculty's perspective, Faculty Senator Pierzynski described four areas of faculty concern in a letter to the provost on April 21, 1996. First, Pierzynski stated that a "clear separation of the individualized evaluation approach, in which a person is deemed to have either failed to meet, met or exceeded expectations, and the chronic [low] achievement issue is essential." The second point of concern was related to realistic goal setting. The letter outlined two possible situations: a faculty member setting low goals that could easily be exceeded, or at the other end of the spectrum, a department head establishing "unattainable goals that a person would always fail to meet, despite tremendous effort." Third, Pierzynski suggested that the provost had overinterpreted Section C31.5 by construing failure in one critical or essential area to signify "overall" failure. The final concern related to the plan to use faculty evaluations as a mechanism for resource reallocation. Pierzynski stated, "many have expressed concern about flexibility in changing appointments of those who are not performing well in a particular area. Such changes in appointments can influence an entire department if important areas of teaching, research, or extension are not being covered or become the responsibility of a few individuals."

The provost responded four days later, steadfastly maintaining his position. Before discussing the senate's specific concerns, Coffman made two points: "(1) The only new provision in this entire process is the establishment of "minimum standards" called for in C31.5. Everything else is in place. (2) Moving to an individualized system of evaluation is first, and foremost, based upon issues related to resource allocation. . .it is essential to engendering more flexible allocation of time and effort." With these observations, Coffman cut to what he saw as the heart of the matter. The real objective of this new approach was "to optimize the likelihood of all faculty being fully productive, and eliminating waste of resources as represented by underutilized time."

The provost commented on each of the faculty senate's concerns. First, he stated that there was no real separation between individual goals and expectations and the minimum departmental standards because the minimum standards should be "understood in the context of each individual's annual game plan." Regarding the use of the term "overall," the provost maintained the position that unsatisfactory performance in one critical or essential area would lead to a below-standard overall evaluation: "At some point, the degree of inadequacy in a given area of work, essential to the mission of the department, is severe enough that corrective action must be taken. For example, at present, we have individuals who have 20 or 30 percent of their assignment in research, and their research productivity is zero. In most instances, their overall evaluation is described as satisfactory and no action is taken. This should cause the entire evaluation to be below minimum standards."

Taking up the topic of reallocation of time and responsibilities, the provost agreed with Pierzynski that in some cases and some departments, this process would be complex and other faculty work might be affected. He allowed that in some cases, reallocation of time would not be feasible and at that point, a "plan for development of requisite skills [would] be part of the department head's 'suggested course of action to improve the performance of the faculty member.'" Finally, with regard to assuring that realistic goals would be established, the provost noted, "specific safeguards are in place to prevent abuse, and must be observed." These included checkpoints at which a faculty member could see his/her evaluation before it was sent to the next level, and ultimately, to the university's grievance process.

Clarifying C31.5

The discussions between the provost and the faculty leadership continued through the spring term and into the fall of 1996. After months of wrangling over the definition of "overall," and the point at which the policy would be invoked, faculty leaders drafted three addenda to the new policy. On December 10, 1996, the senate approved Sections C31.6, C31.7, and C.31.8 (See Exhibit 3.2). As Kuhlman described it, these measures were added "because some felt a need to limit C31.5."

The issue of separating minimum department standards from individual expectations was addressed in Section C31.6, which states: "'dismissal for cause' in cases of professional incompetence can only be based on departmental guidelines about minimum acceptable levels of performance that apply generally to all members of the department or unit and are distinct from individually determined annual goals." In addition, C31.6 emphasized that minimum acceptable levels of performance and the definition of the term "productivity" would be the province of each department. In fact, departments were given considerable leeway. As noted in Section C31.6, "It is expected that guidelines concerning minimum acceptable levels of productivity will vary considerably from unit to unit."

Section C31.7 explicitly stipulated that before any faculty member could be dismissed for cause, serious attempts at remediation must have taken place. It called for a written record of evaluations signaling deficient performance. Only after these had occurred could the department head and the faculty member agree to a reallocation of responsibilities.

Finally, C31.8 detailed the terminology to be used for annual evaluations, with the term "minimum acceptable levels of productivity" referring to the minimum standards called for in C31.5. When approved in December 1996, the text of C31.8 called for departmental guidelines to "explicitly state the point at which a faculty member's overall performance can bring C31.5 into play. The guidelines should reflect the common and dictionary meaning of 'overall' as 'comprehensive.'" In May 1998, the administration and faculty senate renegotiated this section, softening the language somewhat. Rather than "explicitly state the point" at which C31.5 would be brought into play, the guidelines were required to "clearly explain how the department or unit will determine when a tenured faculty member's low performance in one or more instances fails overall to meet the minimum acceptable level."

Practical Effects

Views among administrators and faculty members varied regarding what the new chronic low achievement policy would accomplish. For Coffman, the policy was a mechanism for "nudging the driftwood into action" and a tool that would allow the university to reallocate faculty time and effort when necessary. The regents also appeared to be pleased with the results. John Welsh, the Executive Director of the Board of Regents, said, "The regents believe that we now have policies in place that will allow for the dismissal of chronic low performers, because there will be a clear, written record of evaluation and efforts toward remediation."

Kuhlman viewed the new system and policy as "a success already, because I see a change in attitude. You can no longer go to the department head and say, 'I'm working on a book.' Now you can expect to be asked when it will be finished and how it's being used to enhance teaching." Another former faculty senate president, Havlin, spoke proudly of C31.5: "We stood up and said unproductive faculty members are unacceptable. We stood up and did something about it."

Others predicted that the new policy would have very little effect on the way faculty conduct their work. Instead, they said it had symbolic and political value. Pierzynski predicted that C31.5 would not bring about any major changes. "What the university got out of this is good public relations," he commented. Another faculty senate member called the policy "something to impress the legislature. It's hard for me to see any other major benefit."

Neither the faculty nor the administration or board expected the chronic low achievement policy to produce large numbers of pink slips. In fact, the provost estimated that there might be as few as three to five dismissals over ten years. Welsh, the executive director of the board, predicted that fewer than ten professors would be terminated for cause over that time. He asserted that the regents' "genuine objective is improvement, not dismissal. They are interested in using it as leverage."

By spring 1998, departments had identified seven cases in which faculty members were not meeting the department's definition of minimum acceptable levels of productivity. Specifically, none were producing research. Of the seven, one faculty member chose to retire, two have undergone a reallocation of efforts, two developed remedial plans of action, and another two improved their performance sufficiently to meet the minimum departmental standards. If any of these faculty members fails to meet standards in 1999, the C31.5 remediation process could come into play.

Questions on the Horizon

In April 1998, as K-State's departments continued to develop and refine new evaluation formats and minimum performance standards in consultation with Provost Coffman, some faculty leaders reflected on the results of their work and the questions it raised about the future.

One question was whether the board of regents would be satisfied with an approach that encourages remediation and would likely produce few, if any, pink slips. Had the faculty adequately shored up the dike, was it buying time, or could it be sowing the seeds of further intervention by the board?

Others asked whether the new policy would be effective with such disparate standards among the departments. Was it fair and feasible for some departments to have explicit and stringent standards while others were more nebulous and lenient? What would happen if faculty members in units with rigorous standards suffered adverse consequences, while faculty members in other units did not? And finally, would tenure be safer, or less so, as a result of the policy changes?

In a similar vein, Professor Brad Fenwick in the College of Veterinary Medicine foresaw a possible problem with the concept of reallocating faculty resources. He predicted, "if one person is a mediocre teacher and, as a result of the new process, his appointment is adjusted so that he is assigned 80 percent research and less teaching, then another person in the same department might be ticked off at having to teach an extra course. It might even be incentive for some to teach poorly in order to get out from under a heavy teaching load."

A number of K-State's faculty leaders and administrators offered their early conjectures. Some said, "Yes, we have averted an attempt at establishing post-tenure review." Kuhlman declared, "Tenure has not been challenged. Rather, the ability to use tenure as a shield from productivity and accountability has been challenged." An administrator commented, "The C31.5 process saved the university from evaluating every single faculty member in a full post-tenure review process by only dealing with chronic low achievers." Others disagreed. Professor Hamilton remarked, "Tenure is now *less* secure—and the university needs tenure to attract a high-quality faculty. Now we are at risk of opening the door to an assault on tenure." For many, however, the effect of the chronic low achievement policy on tenure remained an open question—one that only time and future events will answer.

Discussion Questions

1. Does the passage of Sections C31.5, C31.6, C31.7, and C31.8 adequately address the board of regents' concern about faculty performance and accountability? Why or why not?

2. Does the fact that Sections C31.5–C31.8 are implemented primarily on a departmental level make it more or less likely that potential faculty productivity problems will be identified and corrected?

3. Did the passage and implementation of Sections C31.5–C31.8 result in a good outcome at K-State? Why or why not?

4. What is your overall assessment of K-State's approach to organizational change? What elements of their change strategy
are most significant to you? Why?

Recommended Background Readings

Centra, John A. (1993). *Reflective Faculty Evaluation: Enhancing Teaching and
Determining Faculty Effectiveness.* San Francisco: Jossey-Bass.
Chait, Richard P. (1998). "Post-Tenure Review of Department," in *Ideas in Incu-
bation: Three Possible Modifications to Traditional Tenure Policies.* Washing-
ton, D.C.: American Association for Higher Education, pp. 13–20.
Goodman, Madeleine J. (1994). "The Review of Tenured Faculty at a Research
University: Outcomes and Appraisals." *The Review of Higher Education*
18(1): 83–94.
Licata, Christine M., and Joseph C. Morreale, (1997). *Post-Tenure Review: Poli-
cies, Practices, Precautions.* New Pathways Working Paper Series, Inquiry
#12, Washington, D.C.: American Association for Higher Education.
Seldin, Peter (1990). *How Administrators Can Improve Teaching: Moving from
Talk to Action in Higher Education.* San Francisco: Jossey-Bass.

Exhibit 3.1. Memorandum on Faculty Evaluation Recommendations

March 23, 1995

M E M O R A N D U M

TO: Members, Council of Presidents
FROM: Stephen M. Jordan, Executive Director
RE: Faculty Evaluation Recommendations

At the March 16, 1995 Board meeting, the Board of Regents acted on
the one remaining recommendation pertaining to faculty evaluation.
The recommendations adopted in December 1994 and March 1995
supplement recommendations adopted in April 1992. I have attached
copies of the recommendations the Board expects to be implemented in
this important area of our accountability to the public. Please note that

Exhibit 3.1. Memorandum on Faculty Evaluation Recommendations, cont'd.

the Board expects a report on the implementation of these recommendations in May 1996. I have also enclosed a draft of the student perceptions of instruction survey instrument the Board endorsed in March. The councils should react to this draft prior to the Board's consideration of it in May. Once it is adopted, each institution will need to develop a plan to implement it in the 1995–1996 academic year.

cc: Members, Kansas Board of Regents
     Members, Council of Chief Academic Officers
     Members, Council of Faculty Senate Presidents

FACULTY EVALUATION RECOMMENDATIONS

1a. Teaching faculty should be rated by students at least once a year, on a form that is controlled for student motivation and other possible bias. The form should contain directions which indicate how the information is used, and the forms should be administered and collected under controlled conditions that assure students' anonymity. Each academic unit should determine the student rating form to be used by its faculty that conform to the above guidelines.

1b. Multiple sources of information should be gathered to evaluate teaching. Sources of information might include the content of the course, its design and presentation. For example, (a) syllabi, examinations and samples of graded exams, textbooks, etc. might be evaluated by peers for their suitability and coherence, (b) videos of class presentations might be viewed by peers or the department chair to evaluate presentation of material, etc.

Units should be encouraged to develop a comprehensive, flexible approach to teaching evaluation that includes several types of evidence that can be collected, presented and evaluated as a portfolio. Student ratings of teaching should be an important part of this portfolio; they are nevertheless only one part. Peer evaluation, defined as a comprehensive, critical review by knowledgeable colleagues of each faculty member's entire range of teaching activities, should be the foundation of the university's teaching evaluation program. No

Exhibit 3.1. Memorandum on Faculty Evaluation Recommendations, cont'd.

single course of information, including ratings by students, should be taken at face value, but rather should be interpreted by those peers who are in the best position to understand this evidence and to place it in the appropriate academic context. Departments should be encouraged to use additional tools such as exit interviews and graduate interviews and surveys to obtain information about teaching effectiveness.

2a. All department chairs should participate in the evaluation of faculty and meet with faculty individually as needed to discuss the evaluation. Institutions should enhance opportunities for the preparation of department chairs for work in departmental administration, particularly as that relates to the evaluation of faculty and the allocation of faculty effort as in (4).

2b. At the beginning of each academic year, representatives from Student Governance on each campus should have the opportunity to meet with campus representatives from Academic Affairs or their designees to discuss the operation of student ratings of teaching. Ratings of individual faculty are not an appropriate subject in such discussions.

3. Instruments to measure student ratings of instruction should solicit, at a minimum, student perspectives on (a) the delivery of instruction, (b) the assessment of learning, (c) the availability of the faculty members to students, and (d) whether the goals and objectives of the course were met. Printed directions on the rating scale should indicate that the information will be used by the individual faculty member to improve his or her instruction. The department, college and university will also use the information to enhance teaching effectiveness. The forms should be determined, administered, and collected under controlled conditions that assure student anonymity, as indicated in Recommendations 1a and 1b.

4. Based upon institutional and departmental goals, tenured and tenure-track faculty should meet with their department chair individually to allocate the amount of effort that faculty member will devote to teaching, research and service. A reduction of effort in one area should

Exhibit 3.1. Memorandum on Faculty Evaluation Recommendations, cont'd.

be made up by augmentation in another. Merit evaluation of faculty should follow this agreement. These agreements should reflect varying emphases at different times within a faculty member's career. Teaching should be evaluated as rigorously as research.

5. All campuses should insure that each school or college develops a plan to financially recognize faculty who are promoted.

6. In FY 1995, data should be provided on the number and percentage of faculty who received 0% to 1% for the past three consecutive years, and the percentage of all faculty who received a 0% and 1% raise in each of the three past years. This information must be viewed in the context of the total dollars available for merit raises; therefore, the amount of General Fund increase for merit raises should also be given for each of the past three years.

7a. Each campus should i) provide assistance for faculty renewal and development, ii) define chronic low performance, and iii) examine dismissal policies to include chronic low performance, *despite all assistance*, as an indicator of incompetence.

7b. Each institution should provide information to the Board on efforts to improve teaching. The Board will distribute with student ratings scales a one-page survey of student perceptions of instruction. The survey will be collected separately from the student ratings scales used in the evaluation of faculty. The survey will be used to demonstrate student attitudes toward instruction at the Regents universities.

The Regents universities should provide the Board with a report by June 1996 on the implementation of the recommendations adopted in December 1994 and March 1995.

ADOPTED BY THE KANSAS BOARD OF REGENTS, MARCH 16, 1995.

Exhibit 3.2. Excerpt from the Kansas State University Faculty Handbook, Section C: Faculty Identity, Employment, Tenure

C31.6 Section C31.5 is about revocation of tenure in individual cases. Tenure is essential for the protection of the independence of the teaching and research faculty in institutions of higher learning in the United States. Decisions about revocation of tenure, especially if the grounds are professional incompetence, should not be exclusively controlled or determined by and should not be unduly influenced by single individuals without input from faculty. Moreover, "dismissal for cause" in cases of professional incompetence can only be based on departmental guidelines about minimum-acceptable levels of performance that apply generally to all members of the department or unit and are distinct from individually determined annual goals. Consequently, C31.5 establishes a departmental and faculty procedure for the decision about the revocation of tenure for professional incompetence. It is not the purpose of C31.5 to promote, endorse, encourage, or to have any stand whatsoever on the definition of "productivity," its relation to publication, or the proper relationship between measurable definitions of productivity and an intellectual University environment that is favorable to substantive scholarship, long-range projects, or critical and creative thinking. These are matters that C31.5 leaves to the department or unit to consider in "developing a set of guidelines describing the minimum-acceptable level of productivity for all applicable areas of responsibility." These minimum standards are not the same as those referred to in C31.1 or C41.1. It is expected that guidelines concerning minimum-acceptable levels of productivity will vary considerable from unit to unit. Not only disciplinary differences but differences in philosophies of departmental administration are appropriate. What is not appropriate is the undue protection of non-contributing members of the faculty.

C31.7 Prior to the point at which "dismissal for cause" is considered under C31.5, other less drastic actions should have been taken. In most cases, the faculty member's deficient performance ("below expectations" or worse) in one or more areas of responsibility will have been noted in prior annual evaluations. At that point, the first responsibility of the head of the department or unit is to determine explicitly whether the duties assigned to the faculty member have been equitable in the context

Exhibit 3.2. Excerpt from the Kansas State University Faculty Handbook, Section C: Faculty Identity, Employment, Tenure, cont'd.

of the distribution of duties within the unit and to correct any inequities affecting the faculty member under review. Second, the head of the department or unit should have offered the types of assistance indicated in C30.3. Referral for still other forms of assistance (e.g., medical or psychological) may be warranted. Third, if the deficient performance continues in spite of these efforts and recommendations, the department head and the faculty member may agree to a reallocation of the faculty member's time so that he/she no longer has duties in the area(s) of deficient performance. Of course, such reallocation can occur only if there are one or more areas of better performance in the faculty member's profile and if the reallocation is possible in the larger context of the department's or unit's mission, needs, and resources.

C31.8 To help clarify the relationship between annual evaluations for merit, salary, and promotion and evaluations that could lead to C31.5, the following recommendations are made:

   a. When annual evaluations are stated in terms of "expectations," then the categories should include at least the following: "exceeded expectations," "met expectations," "fallen below expectations but has met minimum-acceptable levels of productivity," and "fallen below minimum-acceptable levels of productivity," with the "minimum-acceptable levels of productivity" referring to the minimum standards called for in C31.5.

   b. The department's or unit's guidelines for "minimum-acceptable levels of productivity" should explicitly state the point at which a faculty member's overall performance can bring C31.5 into play. The guidelines should reflect the common and dictionary meaning of "overall" as "comprehensive," which may be based on any of the following:

     1. A certain percentage of total responsibilities

     2. Number of areas of responsibility

     3. Weaknesses not balanced by strengths

     4. Predetermined agreements with the faculty member about the relative importance of different areas of responsibility

Table 3.1. Minimum Performance Standards

	Department in Natural Sciences	Department in Agriculture	Department in Social Sciences
Overall Concept	The department developed a proportionality system that accounts for differences in assigned effort to teaching, research, extension, and service (0 percent to 100 percent in a given area). Faculty are rated on a five-point performance scale (1=unsatisfactory, 5=excellent). Performance ratings are multiplied by the proportion of effort assigned (for example, a 70 percent teaching assignment rated at 3.6 would be calculated as 3.6 x 0.7). A grand score is obtained by adding the ratings for each area. A final score is obtained by adjusting the grand score by the faculty member's salary relative to other salaries in the department. "A faculty member with a higher salary is expected to have a proportionally higher productivity."	The department head assigns a score for each performance category (including nondirected service for all and extension, teaching, research, and directed service according to the individual appointment). The department head subjectively determines levels of accomplishment based on careful consideration of standards for particular criteria in each category. A five-point rating scale is used in which 1=unsatisfactory and 5=excellent. After rating a faculty member on each criterion, the head determines an overall rating on a scale of 0 to 100 in each category. The department guideline states that "faculty who receive a performance rating of less than 60 in teaching, research, extension, or directed service fail to achieve the minimal acceptable level of productivity."	The statements below comprise the department's definition of minimum performance standards.
Teaching	Minimum expectations are "one course taught every 4 years for each 0.1 appointment assigned to teaching. . . with TEVAL scores averaging 2.5 (on a scale of 1–5 with 5 as best) . . . Consideration is given to those classes that do not fill	The minimum standard is an overall rating of 60 in teaching. Examples of criteria and standards for teaching include: student evaluations; TEVAL scores; evaluations by head or assistant head (classroom visits, review of teaching materials);	The minimum standard is stated as: "Fulfills assigned teaching duties."

	for reasons beyond the control of the teacher. . .or for other special reasons."	and the quantity and quality of graduate academic advising based on interviews conducted by department head.	
Research and Publication	"For research appointments of 0.7 and above, two refereed articles over the past 4 years is considered a minimal expectation. For research appointments of 0.1 or 0.2 (primarily Extension faculty) one refereed article over the past 5 years is considered a minimal expectation."	The minimum standard is an overall rating of 60 for research. Criteria and standards include: level of research focus and aggressiveness in attaining goals; quantity and quality of refereed publications; and level of extramural funding.	The minimum standard is stated as: "Progress shown."
Extension	Minimum expectations for extension appointments are an "average score of at least 3 (on a scale of 1–5, with 5 as best) on the annual County Agent evaluation of their performance," which examines the quantity, quality, and reputation of their work.	The minimum standard is a rating of 60 for extension. Criteria and standards for extension include quantity and quality of program development and implementation; peer evaluations of meetings, tours, or demonstrations; level of teamwork and client relationships; and quantity and quality of extension publications.	Not rated.
Service	Not rated.	The minimum standard for nondirected service is a rating of 60. Criteria and standards for nondirected service include contributions through committee assignments; participation in profession-based service and recognition; professional contributions to government or civic groups; and the extent of private consulting activities.	Minimum standards are stated as: "Departmental and university service: Carries share of duties." "Professional service: Participates actively in the profession." "Community service: Responds to requests for service from off campus."

4

Olivet College

Aligning Faculty Employment Policies with an Evolving Mission

William T. Mallon

In fall 1994, President Michael Bassis informed faculty members that he would support a return to a traditional tenure system, which had been abandoned twenty years earlier for a system of five-year renewable contracts. "It's not that I was a huge advocate of traditional tenure, although I do think it has served American higher education well," recalled Bassis. "In the case of Olivet, the evaluation system under five-year contracts was not working. We needed some new mechanism for reviewing and evaluating faculty work."

Despite the faculty's initial flurry of activity on a proposal and board approval for the concept, by spring 1999, the faculty had not carried the initiative forward, and the college still had not implemented traditional tenure.

William T. Mallon prepared this case under the supervision of James P. Honan, lecturer on education, Harvard Graduate School of Education, as the basis for class discussion rather than to illustrate either effective or ineffective handling of an administrative situation.

This case was prepared for the Project on Faculty Appointments and funded by the Pew Charitable Trusts. © 2000 by the President and Fellows of Harvard College. No part of this publication may be reproduced, stored in a retrieval system, used in a spreadsheet, or transmitted in any form by any means—electronic, mechanical, photocopying, recording, or otherwise—without the permission of the Project on Faculty Appointments at the Harvard Graduate School of Education.

Olivet College

Located in a small town forty miles south of Lansing, Michigan, Olivet opened for classes in 1844. A college history reads: "Eleven years after founding Oberlin College, 'Father' John J. Shipherd led a band of 39 missionaries to create a college and a village in the wilderness of Southern Michigan in 1844. Remembering that the Biblical Mount of Olives was a center of piety, morality, and learning, the missionaries named both the college and the village Olivet."

Olivet has a long tradition of educational innovation. It was founded as the second coeducational college in the nation (Oberlin was the first) and immediately opened its doors to all races. It became a leader in literary societies in the mid- to late-1800s; the oldest collegiate sorority in the United States was founded at Olivet in 1847. Between 1934 and 1944, the college earned a national reputation as home to a prestigious writers' conference, with literary giants such as Gertrude Stein and Ezra Pound regular visitors to campus. Its curriculum was patterned after the Oxford model.

Like many small liberal arts colleges, Olivet has a long history of difficult fiscal circumstances, with strong dependence on enrollment and tuition while also providing high levels of financial aid to students in need. Enrollment reached a record high of 850 residential students in 1976, followed by a precipitous decline in enrollment in 1977 to nearly 350 students. By the 1980s, after years of stagnant enrollment, Olivet was in a period of financial and academic decline. Enrollment bottomed out in 1983 and began to increase slowly from 1984 on, but stagnated again in the late 1980s. The music department exemplified this intellectual and physical lifelessness. By the end of the 1980s, the conservatory was an abandoned building and the music curriculum was "moribund," according to an administrator.

Faculty Appointment Policy

Olivet offered traditional, continuous tenure prior to 1974. According to long-time faculty members, the tenure-granting process was without application, procedures, or peer review. "Back then, it was loosely offered," said Professor Don Walker. "The president would just decide who got it. Faculty members would find out they got tenure when it appeared on their contract."

In 1973–1974, the faculty voted thirty to five in favor of replacing continuous tenure with a system of five-year contracts, commonly referred to as "term tenure" or "multiyear contracts." Ray Loeschner, the president, was a new young leader who, according to several faculty members, believed that the elimination of tenure would make the college more efficient. He was concerned with the possibility of the faculty becoming tenured in. "He made the case that tenure could cause the college to become top heavy," recalled Professor Don Rowe.

Professors who had already received traditional tenure retained that status. Faculty were split in their reaction to the announcement that tenure was being replaced with term contracts. Professor Rowe said, "I was surprised that the faculty gave in as easily as they did. One reason was that everyone was aware of the college's continual financial situation, which has always been precarious. In other colleges, faculty can afford to be antagonistic. Here, you can see the whole boat, from one side to the other. Faculty accepted the president's rationale." Professor Walker said, "Faculty voted to relinquish tenure because it was this or nothing. Most faculty at the time didn't have Ph.D.'s. They didn't have other options."

Since 1974, Olivet has operated under the five-year contract policy. (See Exhibit 4.1 for the five-year "tenure" policy document.) Junior faculty served a five-year probationary period consisting of a one-year, then a two-year, then another two-year contract, followed by a review by the Rank, Tenure, and Promotion (RTP) Committee and by the administration. Successful candidates were then offered a five-year contract with review at the end of the five-year period. Olivet's "five-year tenure" system had no up-or-out provision. Instead, "failure to attain tenure when first eligible does not necessarily mean non-reappointment, nor does it mean that tenure could not be granted at a later date" (Olivet College Five-Year "Tenure" Policy, Faculty Handbook, 1987, p. T-1).

"It's not that bad a system," declared Professor Rowe. "A lot of faculty have the mistaken idea that tenure is job security. At a place like this, which is tuition dependent and enrollment driven, it's not."

The shift away from traditional tenure attracted external attention in 1980. The American Association of University Professors (AAUP) censured Olivet for the manner in which two faculty members were terminated. In its report, the AAUP also asserted that the five-year term contract policy had "an adverse impact" on academic freedom and faculty worklife. As of 1999, the college still remained on the association's list of censured institutions.

Commentators reported that the five-year contract system contributed to a "devil's bargain" between the faculty and administration in the 1980s. "The academic dean never bucked the RTP committee in the 1980s and early 1990s," reported Don Tuski, who was a student at Olivet from 1981 to 1985 and later returned as a staff member, professor, and academic administrator. "Although they worked very hard at their teaching and cared about their students, some faculty would not have been tenurable in a traditional sense. The lack of a terminal degree or publishing record on the part of some of the faculty would also have made it difficult for them to achieve traditional tenure." Because only a few faculty members were dismissed under the contract system, most faculty referred to the system as de facto tenure. Between 1980 and 1990, average faculty attrition was 22.4 percent: some 200 faculty came and went during this period. The reality is that those who got through the first five years stayed. The 200 who did not were exposed to a variety of pressures during their first years at the college and did not stay long enough to get into the pipeline.

Crisis and Response

The slow decline of the institution in the 1980s culminated in a cataclysmic crisis in April 1992, when a brawl involving white and black students garnered widespread national media attention for the college. "We were trashed by the media," recalled Professor Rowe. "They ate us alive." In June, thirty-six of the college's forty-six faculty voted no confidence in Donald Morris, Olivet's president of fifteen years. In August, Morris resigned.

An internal college document reported: "Like many small colleges during the 1980s, Olivet failed to adapt to mounting pressures for change. It remained stagnant and failed to acknowledge growing problems of demographics, finances, academic quality, and intergroup relations. Negative publicity from the campus racial incident of 1992 put the college into crisis. A frank assessment of these problems caused the board as well as key faculty and alumni leaders to acknowledge the need for comprehensive change and to seek new presidential leadership to lead the process ("Creating a Model of Institutional Transformation" [internal college document], May 1996, p. 3).

Michael Bassis, formerly executive vice president and provost of Antioch College, assumed the presidency of Olivet in August 1993. In his first year, Bassis eliminated a million-dollar deficit, created an African American cultural center and a student advisor staff position for African American students, and developed a set of institutional priorities, including academic distinctiveness, diversity, community, fiscal integrity, and operating effectiveness.

Bassis also charged the faculty with redesigning the basic educational purposes of the college. Three months later, the faculty presented a new vision statement, Education for Individual and Social Responsibility (see Exhibit 4.2). The vision statement was endorsed by the Olivet faculty on December 6, 1993, and unanimously approved by the board of trustees on January 29, 1994.

An internal document reads:

> Moving beyond the lofty rhetoric of the vision statement, the faculty then specified in precise terms five sets of learning outcomes—each of which were derived from the vision statement—and which define skills and orientations that all Olivet students must acquire and demonstrate prior to

graduation. They include communication skills, reasoning skills, individual responsibility, social responsibility, and skills particular to one's chosen major.

Building on this momentum, the faculty then redesigned the educational program of the college to produce the kind of learning called for in the vision statement and specified in the learning outcomes. The crucial change in this new educational delivery system, known as *The Olivet Plan*, is the focus on student learning rather than on delivering courses, credits, and grades. A redesigned curriculum and multiple opportunities for learning beyond the classroom are both seen as important ways for students to develop competence in the learning outcomes required for graduation.

Exhibit 4.3 describes the elements of the Olivet Plan.

Part of the Olivet Plan involved a modification of the roles of faculty, administrators, and staff. According to a college document, the "multiple opportunities for learning beyond the classroom" meant that: "As we move toward the learning paradigm, putting increased value on the learning that takes place beyond the classroom, we find the traditional differences in the roles and responsibilities of faculty and staff have become blurred. We believe the following must be addressed. . . (1) Definitional issues. How do we overcome traditional hierarchies and celebrate the special roles of the staff in the life of the learning community? (2) Community governance. What is the role of the faculty, staff, and student senates? Should we shift our internal dynamic toward a single governance structure?"

As the Olivet Plan was implemented in the mid-1990s, some administrators, faculty, and staff pursued the idea of "community governance." Under this model, one governing organization would replace the existing structure of separate senates for faculty, staff, and students. "Community governance upset the traditional dichotomy between faculty and staff," said an administrator. "If everyone is an educator, people began to wonder why some of us, namely the faculty, have prerogatives that others of us don't."

Tenure Put Back on the Table

In 1994, during the initial stages of transforming the college's mission, curricula, and educational priorities and practices, a faculty member broached the issue of tenure during a meeting with President Bassis and the RTP Committee. "Someone asked Bassis off the cuff if he would support returning to tenure," said Professor Rowe. "He responded, 'Sure, I'll be willing to go along with that.' I think his response surprised a number of people. While some faculty from time to time groused about the lack of traditional tenure, there had never been a formal movement on the part of faculty or administration to reinstitute tenure."

Bassis recalled several reasons for agreeing to consider a return to traditional tenure:

I was working with the faculty RTP Committee because evaluation and promotion policies had been sloppy for a very long time. I believed that if, together, we could develop a new policy that was clear in expectations and procedures for evaluating faculty work, then I was willing to support a traditional tenure system. But, those two characteristics—clear expectations and systematic evaluation procedures—had to be part of the bargain.

The status quo clearly was not working, and I was convinced that a strong faculty was essential for a strong college. The college needed to ask a lot from the faculty and the faculty a lot from the college.

I saw tenure as a device to move the college into the mainstream. But, more importantly, I also saw it was an incentive for faculty to more greatly participate in the life of the college.

Some faculty members had a slightly different interpretation of the president's use of tenure as an "incentive." Said Professor Tuski, "I think the president realized that the faculty was beaten up in the 1980s, and they needed to be legitimized, more professionalized. One way of doing that was tenure. But I also think Bassis wanted to gain political clout with the faculty because he was asking them to do a lot with transforming the college. It was a political offering from him."

James Halseth, whom Bassis hired as the dean of the college in 1994, noted a similar reason for the reinstatement of tenure. "It was related to morale. Michael sensed that the faculty was demoralized and isolated from the rest of academe. Tenure would create a greater sense of professionalism and invite the college into a national conversation. Our vision was to recapture and renew the college's proud, impressive legacy. To do that, we needed to infuse the faculty with a rejuvenated spirit. Tenure was all bound up in that."

Don Tuski also believed that the president's desire for tenure was related to faculty recruitment. "We were thin on faculty with terminal degrees. Barely 40 percent of faculty had terminal degrees in 1993. People didn't publish. We had a heavy teaching load. I think we were getting people with master's degrees rather than Ph.D.'s because, in part, of the lack of tenure. But at Olivet, teaching is the most important thing."

Another of the administration's concerns was the AAUP's censure. When Bassis and Halseth arrived at Olivet, they made inquiries about removing the college from the AAUP's censure list. The association stipulated that the college would have to pay restitution to the dismissed professors and institute a traditional tenure policy. "Removing the college from the AAUP's censure list," reported Halseth, "would have been one of the byproducts of tenure, although it was not the reason for doing it."

Halseth contacted the AAUP and ordered multiple copies of the Red Book.[1] "We were going to have the most traditional tenure system in the country."

Not everyone viewed the offer to return to tenure in a positive light. Even though President Bassis had announced that no faculty would be dismissed because of the efforts to reinvent the college's curriculum, some faculty automatically viewed the initiative with skepticism born out of their mistrust for all things administrative—a holdover from the relationship between the faculty and previous administrations. "This was an adversarial culture," observed Dean Halseth.

Said Professor Walker, "Some faculty saw the new president as a house cleaner. They thought he was going to come in and sweep out a lot of the long-time faculty members. So, when he raised the possibility of returning to a tenure system, they viewed it quite suspiciously. They saw it as a ploy to raise faculty evaluation standards. By no means was this an idea with which all faculty agreed."

Trustees "raised a few eyebrows" when they heard about the possibility of returning to tenure, said President Bassis. "I did not consult with the board about this idea. I never had a policy discussion with them. It never got to that point." However, according to Dean Halseth, the board supported the idea "because they wanted to mollify the president." The board indicated that they would support a return to tenure only if it included a periodic review of senior faculty. A faculty member observed that the board rallied behind Bassis' attempts to reinvigorate the college: "They would have given him anything he wanted."

The RTP Committee's Tenure Proposal and the Handbook Revision

Once Bassis signaled that he was willing to support a tenure system, the RTP Committee developed a tenure proposal during the 1994–95 academic year. It consisted of a two-track system: all current faculty members would have the option of remaining on five-year term contracts or migrating to the tenure system, while new junior faculty would be placed on a tenure track.

Faculty proposed the two-track system because many of them felt threatened by a traditional tenure system. "After six months of studying the possibilities," said Professor Tuski, "many faculty realized that traditional tenure would be unattainable for people without Ph.D.'s. The Ph.D. is the norm for tenure." Dean Halseth noted, "A lot of people were fearful of an up-or-out system."

For some faculty, the reality of a more rigorous evaluation cooled their initial enthusiasm for a tenure policy. Professor Rowe maintained, "A lot of people calling for tenure assumed there would be the same type of review as there was under the five-year contract system. They didn't realize the process would be more stringent."

Some faculty said the administration shelved their proposal. "They didn't like the two-track system because faculty would have the option of remaining under the current system, so the faculty's proposal was scuttled," said Professor Walker. Bassis stated that he wanted all faculty to be subject to greater expectations under a new faculty employment system: "I told the faculty that the board would never accept a traditional tenure system that grandfathered in anybody. Everyone would have to start from scratch and undergo a tenure review. I actually didn't consult with the board on that—I used it as a threat. I saw a potentially huge problem if a large proportion of the faculty, probably around two-thirds, were grandfathered into tenure. I needed their continued energy for the transformation of the college's curriculum and educational policies. The expectations for faculty evaluation were very low and fuzzy. I wanted a much higher level of expectation."

In 1995, Bassis hired a nationally known consultant to write a new handbook for Olivet, part of which contained a tenure policy. To meet Bassis's expectation, the tenure "phase-in plan" (See Exhibit 4.4) stipulated that all senior-level faculty members (those with seven or more years of service) would undergo a review for tenure: "Should any full-time faculty member not receive a continuous contract after consideration for that status is completed. . . the faculty member will be given one further year. . . to attain that status. . . .

If the faculty member fails to be recommended a second time, a one-year terminal contract for cause will be issued" (Proposed Faculty Handbook, 1995, pp. 123–124).

"By nesting the tenure issue in the context of the handbook revisions," said Professor Walker, "the administration made the tenure issue go away, because senior faculty did not want to be subject to an up-or-out policy."

Dean Halseth attended to different roadblocks:

> For a period of twelve to eighteen months, not much occurred on the part of the faculty. Michael Bassis and I waited for some action. So, we had the idea to write the tenure policy into the handbook, which is why we hired a consultant. We expected the faculty to set up a tenure policy and run with it. Their argument is that they didn't have the time or energy. So, the consultant wrote it. Then, the faculty spent a year arguing about it. Faculty leaders believed that developing a tenure policy would be rancorous. They didn't want that. They chose to do nothing because they didn't want to create rancor.
>
> By 1997, the president and I stopped pushing it. We took the position that we supported a tenure policy, but we would let the idea "percolate" among faculty. Our dilemma was that we preferred the faculty to take ownership of the proposal, but the faculty leadership did not want the struggle and animosity that they thought would inevitably occur.

During this time, Halseth and Bassis became open to the concept of a two-track system. Several faculty worked on contract proposals and new handbook language. However, senior faculty failed to support the concept and the initiative stalled. Bassis framed these delays as a matter of priorities: "We couldn't do everything at once. In the institutional transformation process, there were more important

issues to attend to. Faculty energy was already deployed in other elements of the change. I didn't push tenure to the top of the agenda.
I thought other things were more critical."

One of those more urgent issues at the time was the development of the Olivet Plan. "The changes to the handbook and the
tenure proposal had to go on the back burner," said Professor Tuski.
Other faculty agreed with the president's priorities. "Implementing
the Olivet Plan was like repairing a plane in flight," asserted Professor Rowe. "Tenure was simply put on hold."

Awaiting a New President

Michael Bassis left Olivet in July 1998 to accept a position as the
dean and warden (equivalent to the position of president) of New
College at the University of South Florida. Dean Halseth served as
acting president until July 1999, when he left to become president of
Iowa Wesleyan College. In summer 1999, the college eagerly awaited
its new president, F. J. Talley, formerly the associate provost for academic and student services at Rowan University in New Jersey.

As the campus began preparing for the arrival of the new president, faculty and administrators had divergent opinions about the
future of the tenure initiative:

> *Professor Don Rowe:*
> For a long time, there was simply too much going on.
> We were too overwhelmed with other changes to be
> concerned about tenure. As the dust settles with the
> Olivet Plan and as things normalize, tenure will be put
> back on the table. But, the tenure system will have a
> post-tenure review. When you add financial exigency
> and PTR into the tenure policy, people will see that it's
> not much different than the system we have now. So,
> this could still be derailed by sheer ambivalence on the
> part of the faculty.

Professor Don Walker:
You have to understand the faculty culture here. The racial incident in 1992 was an impetus for monumental change. A lot of new faculty came on board. When Bassis introduced the idea of the Olivet Plan and transforming the paradigm of teaching to a paradigm of learning, the faculty was divided in ways it never before experienced. People who didn't like what was happening left. So, in the last few years, turnover has been so high that many people who were gung-ho about getting tenure are no longer here. Many new faculty don't know the history of what happened several years ago.

Associate Vice President for Academic Affairs Don Tuski:
From an institutional perspective, tenure is not a big issue at the moment because the job market is so tight, plus we offer an opportunity to teach in an environment that is educationally and pedagogically progressive. Olivet doesn't look so bad because prospective faculty members have a lot less choice. A small liberal arts college is pretty good compared to a community college or a one-year post-doc. Most prospective faculty members don't flinch when they find out we don't have traditional tenure.

Former President Michael Bassis:
Tenure wasn't immediately implemented because faculty recognized that there were more important things to do other than tenure. The overhaul to the curriculum was a massive undertaking. There was another issue at play, too. I think when it became apparent that everyone would have had to go through a more rigorous evaluation process, some faculty asked, "Do I really want to bring that on myself?"

Former Dean James Halseth:

Tenure remains an issue in almost everyone's mind. It's not as simple as adopting the Red Book guidelines. The college also has to make a major decision about governance. The organizational culture needs to change. The Olivet Plan is blurring the lines between faculty and staff. We have moved to an idea of community governance. We are exploring the possibility of having one handbook for faculty and staff. For those people who support these changes, there is not that much interest in tenure. There is an interest in breaking down hierarchies.

It is not clear where the new president stands on tenure. He's going to have to deal with the tenure issue when he arrives. But for now, no one knows what he thinks about it, and that works to his advantage.

Redefining Faculty and Staff Roles and Responsibilities

In addition to grappling with questions about tenure policy, Olivet was also engaged in a series of institutional transformation initiatives. A working group of administrators, faculty, staff, students, and trustees called the Olivet Employee Plan Project Group began a series of discussions in 1998 regarding the definition of faculty and staff roles and responsibilities at Olivet and the extent to which employee roles and responsibilities were aligned with the principles of the Olivet College mission and vision, the Olivet Plan, and the Olivet College Compact. (See Exhibit 4.5.)

The overall purpose of the group's work was to attempt to equalize the roles and stature of all Olivet employees involved with teaching and learning. The project group attempted to overcome traditional hierarchies that exist among faculty and staff by acknowledging and recognizing the important role that all college employees play in the development of student learning while maintaining equilibrium between the unique roles faculty and staff play at the institution. Among the policy questions the project group tried to address were: What criteria should be used to distinguish faculty from staff? What criteria should be used to evaluate employee performance? What are the roles of faculty, staff, and student senates? Should the college develop a unicameral, community governance structure? Should the college have one policy handbook for all employees?

As the answers to these important questions emerge and as decisions regarding faculty tenure policies are made, Olivet College will likely engage in conversations and deliberations that touch on the core values and beliefs of the academy.

References

"Creating a Model of Institutional Transformation" [internal college document], May 1996.
Olivet College Five-Year "Tenure" Policy, 1987.

Endnote

1. The AAUP's *Policy Documents and Reports*, a guide to traditional tenure policy, is known by its distinguishable bright red cover.

Discussion Questions

1. Evaluate Olivet College's three approaches to faculty employment policy. Which one is most effective? Why?

2. In what ways should Olivet College modify its faculty employment policies to align them more closely with the values and concepts inherent in the Olivet Plan and the new vision statement, Education for Individual and Social Responsibility?

3. Should Olivet College return to a system of traditional tenure for faculty? Why or why not?

Recommended Background Readings

Austin, Ann E., R. Eugene Rice, Allen P. Splete, and Associates. (1991). *A Good Place to Work: Sourcebook for the Academic Workplace*. Washington, DC: Council of Independent Colleges.

Breneman, David W. (1997). *Alternatives to Tenure for the Next Generation of Academics*. New Pathways Working Paper Series, Inquiry #14. Washington, DC: American Association for Higher Education.

Chait, Richard P. (1998). *Ideas in Incubation: Three Possible Modifications to Traditional Tenure Policies*. New Pathways Working Paper Series, Inquiry #9. Washington, DC: American Association for Higher Education.

Chait, Richard, and Cathy A. Trower. (1997). *Where Tenure Does Not Reign: Colleges With Contract Systems*. New Pathways Working Paper Series, Inquiry #3. Washington, DC: American Association for Higher Education.

Magrath, C. Peter. (1997). "Eliminating Tenure Without Destroying Academic Freedom." *Trusteeship*, 5(3): 16–19.

Mallon, William T. (2002). "Why Is Tenure One College's Problem and Another's Solution?" In Richard P. Chait, ed., *The Questions of Tenure*. Cambridge, MA: Harvard University Press.

Mangan, Katherine S. (1989). "Four Colleges' Experiences with Alternatives to Traditional Tenure." *The Chronicle of Higher Education*, March 1, p. A10.

Trower, Cathy A. (1996). *Tenure Snapshot*. New Pathways Working Paper Series, Inquiry #2. Washington, DC: American Association for Higher Education.

Yarmolinsky, Adam. (1996). "Tenure: Permanence and Change: A Case for the Flexible Contract." *Change*, 28(3): 16–20.

Exhibit 4.1. Five-Year Tenure Policy (1974–2000)

Tenure Policy*

I. General Statement

A. Tenure at Olivet College is not permanent. It is awarded for a five-year term and is limited to full-time Faculty members.

B. During the fourth year of each five-year tenure, the individual's performance will be reviewed and evaluated. If the individual's

---

*Prior to the adoption of the above policy in March 1974, Olivet College had a policy of lifetime tenure (defined as "tenure to mandatory retirement age"), and some senior members of the full-time faculty are covered by that earlier policy.

Exhibit 4.1. Five-Year Tenure Policy (1974–2000), cont'd.

performance is found to be satisfactory, an additional five-year term will be granted. For Faculty receiving first-time tenure, evaluations will be done in the fifth year of full-time employment.

C. Failure to attain tenure when first eligible does not necessarily mean non-reappointment, nor does it mean that tenure could not be granted at a later date.

D. If the granting or renewal of tenure falls within a period of less than five years before mandatory retirement, the tenure will be granted only until the retirement age is reached.

E. Both the granting and renewal of tenure will depend upon satisfactory performance in teaching, advising, performing (where relevant), committee work, professional activities, scholarship, and other duties as they may apply. In determining satisfactory performance, the Rank, Tenure, and Promotion Committee will follow the Procedures for Assessing Performance for Full-time Faculty Members (Section Q).

II. Minimum Standards for Awarding Tenure

A minimum of five years of full-time employment at Olivet.

III. Procedure for Awarding Tenure

A. The Chief Academic Officer will furnish the names of all Faculty members who will be eligible for tenure under the above standards to the Rank, Tenure, and Promotion Committee by October 1. At the same time, each Department Chairperson will be notified of the members of the Department who meet these standards. Thereafter, the review proceeds from the Committee to the Chief Academic Officer to the President, and from the President to the Board of Trustees.

B. Persons eligible for tenure will be considered in March of the year preceding that in which tenure could take effect (i.e. March of the fifth year at Olivet, or thereafter). Should one fail to be recommended for tenure the Committee may recommend: (1) that the Faculty member be given a terminal contract, or (2) that the Faculty member be placed on probationary status and a program be instituted to rectify the specific deficiencies outlined by the

Exhibit 4.1. Five-Year Tenure Policy (1974–2000), cont'd.

Chief Academic Officer and the Rank, Tenure, and Promotion Committee. NO such probationary program may be extended beyond a two-year period. In the event that the Committee and the Chief Academic Officer cannot come to an agreement on a particular case, it will be reviewed by the Faculty Senate whose recommendation will be sent by the Chief Academic Officer, along with his own, to the President, who will formulate his or her recommendation to the Board of Trustees for the final decision. In any case, subject to the President's approval, the Chief Academic Officer retains the right to retain the non-tenured Faculty member on a year-to-year or semester-to-semester basis.

IV. Renewal Procedures

A. Five-year tenured Faculty will be reviewed for possible renewal of tenure during October of the fourth year.

B. If, upon recommendation of the Rank, Tenure, and Promotion committee, the Chief Academic Officer decides not to recommend renewal of tenure, the person will be notified by December 15, and also informed that his or her case may be reconsidered, at the Faculty member's request, at the March meeting of the Committee. If, after review, the decision by the committee and the Chief Academic Officer is still not to recommend renewal of tenure, the Faculty member will be given a final contract in May and a year's termination notice. In exceptional cases, such a Faculty member may be placed on probationary status and a program be instituted to rectify specific deficiencies outlined by the Chief Academic Officer and the Rank, Tenure, and Promotion Committee; no such program may be extended beyond a two-year period. In the event that the Committee and the Chief Academic Officer cannot come to an agreement on a particular case, it will be reviewed by the Faculty Senate, whose recommendation will be sent by the Chief Academic Officer, along with his or her own, to the President, who will formulate his or her recommendation to the Board of Trustees for final decision.

Source: 1987 Faculty Handbook for Policies and Procedures.

Exhibit 4.2. Olivet College: Education for Individual and Social Responsibility

Our Vision

Olivet College is dedicated today, as it was in 1844, to the principle that the future of humanity rests in the hands, hearts, and minds of those who will accept responsibility for themselves and others in an increasingly diverse society. This principle of individual and social responsibility is realized in the context of a distinctive liberal arts experience which nurtures in our students the emergence and development of skills, perspectives, and ethics necessary to better themselves and society. We seek to involve our students in an active academic community which cherishes diversity of thought and expression. In so doing, we will help our students discover ways they can most effectively contribute to the common good.

Our Aspirations

We aspire to provide a campus-wide academic culture such that our students will come to understand the need to serve others as well as themselves, to celebrate both the wealth of human diversity and the bond of human similarity, to care for the earth and all its resources, and to strike a balance among their intellectual, physical, emotional, and spiritual capacities. It is our hope that each graduate will embrace our essential principle in his or her life's work.

Our Commitment

Driven by our academic vision, Olivet College maintains a learning environment that encourages scholastic excellence among students, faculty, and the wider campus community. Students at Olivet College are committed first to their learning. Faculty at Olivet College are committed first to their teaching. And, the institution is committed first to providing the necessary resources and support to achieve these goals both within and beyond the classroom.

Our Heritage

The foundation of our guiding principle was established one hundred and fifty years ago by the founders of Olivet College when they wrote,

"We wish simply to do good to our students, by placing in their hands the means of intellectual, moral and spiritual improvement, and to teach them the divine art and science of doing good to others."

Adopted by the Olivet College Faculty Dec. 6, 1993; adopted by the Olivet College Board of Trustees Jan. 29, 1994.

Exhibit 4.3. The Elements of the Olivet Plan

The Portfolio Program

In the Portfolio Program, every student develops a personal portfolio which included, but is not limited to, such items as: projects, created objects, recorded performances, papers and writing samples, interviews, reading lists, etc. The portfolio provides a mechanism for students to document their skills in the five key groups of educational outcomes. These include communicating, reasoning, working together, and individual and social responsibility.

The First Year Experience

Laying the groundwork for skill enhancement and character formulation, the First Year Experience course orients students to college-level learning in general and to special opportunities for learning at Olivet.

The General Education Program

A sequence of specially designed core courses provides common learning and shared experiences for all students. These courses enable students to build their skills across the full range of important educational outcomes.

Service Learning

Each Olivet student completes a semester-long course that includes community service and guided reflection on that service. The experience of working with others to strengthen a community in need is a powerful way to learn about the value and rewards of service to others and to deepen one's sense of individual and social responsibility.

Learning Communities

Learning communities consist of groups of students enrolling concurrently in three different but thematically linked courses. Here students explore important themes and issues (e.g. the environment) with each other and with the help of experts from beyond the campus.

The Academic Major

All students complete an academic major. The major provides students with a depth of knowledge and skill in their area of special interest.

The Senior Year Experience

The Senior Year Experience includes a Capstone Course, culminating in an independent project; the Senior Portfolio; and Senior Courses, proposed and initiated by the students themselves.

Exhibit 4.3. The Elements of the Olivet Plan, cont'd.

Diversity
Celebrating both the bond of human similarity as well as the wealth of human diversity is a theme that runs throughout all elements of the Olivet Plan.

An Innovative Calendar
Most classes meet only twice each week. Wednesdays are reserved for activities such as Service Learning, Portfolio Assessment, and Learning Communities. The spring semester includes an Intensive Learning Term (ILT) where students may concentrate their attention on a single course of special interest in just over three weeks.

Beyond the Curriculum
Olivet considers extracurricular activities, including jobs, athletics, and campus and community activities, as integral to, not apart from, each student's educational experience.

The Olivet Lecture and Symposium Series
The Series, aptly titled "Responsibility Matters," brings the world to Olivet in the form of distinguished speakers and noted discussions leaders.

**Exhibit 4.4. Tenure Phase-In Plan under
Proposed Faculty Handbook, 1995**

D2.7.3. *Continuous Contract Phase-In Plan 1995–1996 to 1997–1998.*

Full-time faculty with seven or more years of full-time experience at Olivet will be divided into three groups.

    Group A: Twenty plus years of service

    Group B: Eleven plus years of service

    Group C: Eight to ten years of service

    Group A will be reviewed for continuous contract status and for a Senior Faculty Five Year Review during 1995–1996.

    Group B will be reviewed for continuous contract status and for a Senior Faculty Five Year Review in 1996–1997.

    Group C will be reviewed for continuous contract status and for a Senior Faculty Five Year Review in 1997–1998.

**Exhibit 4.4. Tenure Phase-In Plan under
Proposed Faculty Handbook, 1995, cont'd.**

These groups of current faculty can be obtained from the Vice President and Dean of the College.

Should any full-time faculty member not receive a continuous contract after consideration for that status is completed by the Rank, Promotion, and Tenure Committee, the Vice President and Dean of College, the President, and the Board of Trustees, the faculty member will be given one further year through a review the following year to attain continuous status. Should that be obtained the faculty member will have received the Senior Faculty Five Year Review, and be in the five year cycle for further reviews.

If the faculty member fails to be recommended a second time, a one year terminal contract for cause will be issued. The faculty member may grieve the terminal contract prior to starting the contract year under the provisions of Section 2.16.

Those full-time faculty members in their first through sixth years at Olivet will come up for a review for continuous contract status in their sixth year on the faculty. They will follow the same procedures as above for approval or disapproval and will, if disapproved, be able to apply for a review in the following academic year with the same provisions discussed above. Their first Senior Faculty Five Year Review will take place five years after attaining a continuous contract.

Faculty hired full-time after July 1, 1995, will be reviewed in their seventh year for continuous contract status, but if they fail to attain that status they will be given a terminal one year contract without further review.

Exhibit 4.5. The Olivet College Compact

On April 2, 1997, members of the Olivet College Community convened to give further definition to our institutional vision of *Education for Individual and Social Responsibility*. The goal was to formulate a set of principles about what it means to be a responsible member of this college community, principles that would serve as an inspiration and as a guide

Exhibit 4.5. The Olivet College Compact, cont'd.

to students, faculty, staff, administrators and trustees alike. This open and inclusive process produced

The Olivet College Compact

Olivet College is founded on and devoted to student learning, growth and development. The College values diversity within a community built on trust, participation and a sense of pride. As a member of this community, I affirm the following commitments:

I am responsible for my own learning and personal development.

We recognize the critical importance of taking ownership for our learning. We seek to learn from the full range of our experience, to be open to new experiences and new ideas and to continuously pursue excellence and fulfillment in our intellectual, social and spiritual pursuits.

I am responsible for contributing to the learning of others.

Every learner benefits when each shares ideas, insights and experiences with others. We value differences of opinion and perspective as well as open, respectful dialogue about these differences as central to the ongoing learning process.

I am responsible for service to Olivet College and the larger community.

People working together for the common good is a key to growth for both the individual and the community. We commit ourselves to participating in community service and volunteer activities, both on and off campus.

I am responsible for contributing to the quality of the physical environment.

Enhancing environmental quality is critical to the College, the community and ultimately to the survival of our planet. We will act to maintain and improve our facilities and grounds, to enhance the safety, the security and the appearance of our surroundings and to protect the ecology of our larger community.

I am responsible for treating all people with respect.

We aim to create a positive and inclusive campus culture celebrating both the individual and cultural differences which make each of us

Exhibit 4.5. The Olivet College Compact, cont'd.

unique and the similarities which bond us together. We recognize the need to seek to understand others as the first step to developing mutual understanding, caring and respect.

I am responsible for behaving and communicating with honesty and integrity.
We build trust when we communicate openly, when we seek justice and fairness for all people, regardless of role or position, and when we honor our values and commitments in our private as well as public behavior.

I am responsible for the development and growth of Olivet College.
We reach outward and seek to inform, involve and recruit new students, employees and friends who share the vision and principles of Olivet College.

In joining this community, I commit myself to these principles and accept the obligation entrusted to me to foster a culture of responsibility at Olivet College.

Endorsed by the Faculty, the Staff Senate and the Student Senate in May 1997 and by the Board of Trustees in June 1997.

5

University of Central Arkansas

*Transformative Leadership, Premium
Contracts, and a New Identity*

Cheryl Sternman Rule

In an era when some observers assert that college presidents paint with tentative strokes and faint hues, one need only travel to Conway, Arkansas, to discover a different approach to the art of presidential leadership. Here, some thirty miles northwest of Little Rock, Winfred Thompson, president of the University of Central Arkansas (UCA), is working on two large canvases at once, each a dramatic departure from academic convention. Whether the president's innovative style will eventually win critical acclaim, denunciations, or a mix of both remains to be seen. In the meantime, Thompson has attracted national attention, first by instituting a policy to pay faculty a sizable salary premium for forgoing the tenure track, and second by planning to transform UCA into a "charter university" largely free of state regulation.

Cheryl Sternman Rule prepared this case under the supervision of Richard P. Chait, professor of higher education, at the Harvard Graduate School of Education, as the basis for class discussion rather than to illustrate either effective or ineffective handling of an administrative situation.

This case was prepared for the Project on Faculty Appointments and funded by the Pew Charitable Trusts. © 1999 by the President and Fellows of Harvard College. No part of this publication may be reproduced, stored in a retrieval system, used in a spreadsheet, or transmitted in any form or by any means—electronic, mechanical, photocopying, recording, or otherwise—without the permission of the Project on Faculty Appointments at the Harvard Graduate School of Education.

The University and Its Leader

Established in 1907 as the Arkansas State Normal School, the University of Central Arkansas (UCA) enrolls about 9,000 students in 75 undergraduate and 32 graduate programs. The university employs approximately 400 full-time faculty members who hold traditional appointments on and off the tenure-track. Because salaries lag quite far behind the national norm,[1] 46 percent of faculty members opt to teach extra courses in the summer in order to earn extra money.

President Thompson earned his master's and doctorate degrees at the University of Chicago and also holds two law degrees from George Washington University. He served as a congressional aide and as vice chancellor for finance and administration at the University of Arkansas at Fayetteville. His professional career has also included work in development and in the practice of law. Thompson assumed the presidency of UCA in 1988. "My faculty critics would say that I am not really an academic person," he acknowledged.

Thompson's years at UCA have not always been smooth. At one point, he sued the state board of higher education for the right to offer a doctorate in physical therapy. About five years ago, the tenured and tenure-track faculty voted no confidence in him by a one-vote majority.[2] The issues prompting their vote included: Thompson's consolidation of departments where his most persistent critics resided; the fact that Thompson "had been at war with the English Department" over curricular priorities since his arrival at UCA; and the board's decision to renovate the president's house at a cost of $400,000. Having given the vote of no confidence, most faculty were convinced that the board would heed their demands for a new president. Instead, the board extended Thompson's contract and gave him a raise.

Let's Make a Deal

In a front page article on March 18, 1999, the *Boston Globe* reported: "Winfred Thompson wants to make a deal. But caveat emptor, his critics say; what he is selling could destroy the soul of the modern

American university. The deal is this: Every new hire at UCA. . . can get a tenure or a tenure-track position, or a 50% salary premium and a three-year rolling contract. Those on contract can be fired, but they still get two years' notice"[3] (Zernike, 1999, p. A1).

Trained as a lawyer, President Winfred Thompson sometimes likens tenure to the criminal justice system: "All the protections are supposed to protect the innocent, but the ones who actually draw the benefits are often the least productive faculty" (Magner, 1998). In fact, Thompson believes that tenure "acts as a disincentive to productivity and hard work." As a result, he has spent five years thinking up creative ways "to tweak the system a little bit."

A few years before Thompson's proposed "deal," he had suggested extending the probationary period for tenure-track faculty to eight years. The faculty senate was so outraged that its members contacted the AAUP. The proposal failed. Thompson's second idea was to stretch out the promotion process in order "to slow it down." He simply felt that too many people were moving up through the system too quickly. This proposal was also greeted with suspicion. Thompson explained his thinking: "In my own way, I thought tenure ought to be looked at not as a canon to be worshipped but as just another economic factor with costs and benefits to the employee and the institution. . . . Why must the AAUP and the faculty think the *only* way to run higher education is to use the AAUP model from 1915?"

As Don Adlong, an assistant professor of mathematics at UCA for thirty-two years, remarked prophetically, Thompson "was always trying innovative things."

Dropping the Bombshell

When institutional research revealed that the students of non-tenure-track faculty at UCA performed as well as or better on a standardized assessment test than students taught by tenured faculty, Thompson felt the time was right to propose a major change. The president first floated the basic elements of a pay-premium, non-tenure-track policy with select members of the board of trustees. If Thompson had raised the issue at an official board meeting, the entire discussion would have been on the record. Instead, he met with board members individually, thereby keeping his plans relatively quiet. The trustees "were generally favorable" because they "instinctively dislike the notion of tenure." For years, anecdotes abounded about tenured faculty members "seen mowing their lawns at 2:00 P.M." or who "went out bass fishing" during business hours. While some of these rumors were undoubtedly false, Thompson felt that such negative impressions could best be addressed through a shift in policy.

Next, Thompson presented his thinking to the president's cabinet. According to Thompson, the new provost and former dean of natural sciences and mathematics, John Mosbo, "was agreeable to trying out" the new plan.

Without having consulted the faculty before this point, Thompson announced the new tenure plan toward the end of his faculty address opening the 1998–99 academic year.

> [T]oday I am proposing an experiment. Keep in mind, as I continue, that my goal is to recruit and retain the finest possible faculty and staff members and to the extent possible to encourage maximum productivity throughout the course of their careers.
>
> The usual assumption is that universities which offer tenure-track and tenured positions will be more successful in recruiting outstanding faculty members than those who do not. The validity of this assumption is, however, thrown into question by an implicit corollary. That corollary is that non-tenure-track positions are assumed to pay less than tenure-track positions. What I propose, in effect, turns that postulate on its head. . .
>
> Specifically, I propose the following, effective for the fall term, 1999. Where appropriate administrative approvals

have been secured, prospective faculty should be offered the option of employment on a nine-month tenure-track appointment *or* a three-year annually renewable twelve-month non-tenure-track contract. [These non-tenure-track] contracts will include provisions guaranteeing academic freedom in the classroom, protecting all relevant constitutional and statutory rights. . . and, as an incentive, offer a continuing salary not less than the national average for faculty members of the same rank according to the most recent AAUP compilations.

[S]o long as the faculty member's performance is satisfactory and there is a continuing need for the position the contract will "roll over" each year. . . In the absence of serious nonfeasance or malfeasance, the faculty member would always have a minimum of two years' notice for the termination of employment.

Under this alternative, newly appointed assistant professors at UCA would receive twelve-month contracts with salaries at a minimum of 11/9ths of the national average.

The Mechanics of Policy 302

The board of trustees officially adopted Thompson's plan (Policy 302) in March 1999. Policy 302 offers "eligible" faculty recruits a *choice* between 1) a traditional nine-month tenure-track position (with no assured summer teaching) at the "standard" salary *or* 2) a new type of twelve-month non-tenure-track appointment at a salary "at least equal to 11/9 of the national average salary for faculty members in the same rank and discipline."[4] "Eligible" faculty are individuals qualified for a tenure-track appointment based on educational background (such as a terminal degree in their field) and prior experience.

The new non-tenure-track appointments differ from traditional tenure-track appointments in several important respects:

- The appointments are for three years, and the contracts "roll over" each year if "the faculty member has
  rendered satisfactory service" and "the university antic-
  ipates a continuing need for the position." If not, the
  faculty member can be terminated with two years'
  notice.

- Faculty members would be required to teach year-
  round, including during the summer session. Currently,
  faculty members on traditional appointments, except
  for department chairs, are not required to teach over
  the summer.

- The salary would be at a premium (11/9 of the national
  average).

- The teaching load would vary from thirty to thirty-six
  credit hours per year as opposed to a twenty-four credit
  hour load for tenure-track faculty.

- Faculty members on multiyear appointments would be
  guaranteed the same academic freedom protections as
  tenured faculty, including "the ability to redress a grievance with the academic freedom committee."

Faculty Reaction

When Thompson announced Policy 302, faculty reacted with more
confusion and resignation than outrage. Linda Shalik, chair of the
Department of Occupational Therapy and member of the faculty
senate, noted, "The president's speech was about attracting the best
and brightest faculty from around the nation. On the other hand, it
was about cost saving. So there's been a lot of confusion about the
goal. It's still not clear what the ultimate purpose of the policy is."
Shalik and Don Adlong both agreed that the formal faculty gover-

nance structure played little role in the shaping of the policy. Thompson's speech proposing the policy "was a total surprise," Shalik said. Adlong agreed: "He got up and just dropped this bombshell."

But both David Skotko, chair of the Department of Psychology and Counseling, and Venita Lovelace-Chandler, chair of the Department of Physical Therapy, saw merit in the new policy. Skotko said: "I was trying to recruit two faculty members back to the campus. They were very research-oriented and had very marketable credentials. They didn't need the security of a tenure-track position because they were so well published, so the new policy was helpful to me as an incentive. I was able to offer them salaries in excess of what they would have earned on the tenure-track. They could go anywhere. In fact, the mobility [afforded by the new policy] was attractive to them."

Lovelace-Chandler expressed similar enthusiasm about the new option: "I love choices. Plus, the tenure-track faculty in my department think this is great because they won't have to compete with these new faculty for the tenure slots."

For Skotko and Lovelace-Chandler, the policy affords department chairs great flexibility. Because the policy "has not been clearly articulated," the chairs, according to Skotko, have great leeway in shaping potential offers. "I decide whether to offer [new faculty] the choice. And I don't have to justify withholding that choice from a particular candidate," explained Skotko. Lovelace-Chandler agreed. "We shape these offers in the way we want them to be shaped. We read the policy the way we want to read it," she said.

Other chairs and faculty members viewed Policy 302 as more vague than flexible. One department chair noted, "I'm not sure the mechanics of the policy have been clearly articulated." Bob Willenbrink, chair of the Department of Speech, Theater, and Mass Communication agreed: "My initial difficulty with the policy is that when the president proposed it at the faculty meeting, it was ill-defined." One tenured faculty member asked, "My understanding was that this policy was supposed to save money, but how could it?"

These questions and others inspired a report entitled, "Questions, Concerns, and Implementation Issues about Three-Year Rolling Contracts as an Option to Tenure." According to Shalik, a member of the committee appointed by the provost to author the report, "Our charge was to look at what questions needed to be answered in order for the policy to be implemented successfully." The report raised several concerns, and then posed 123 questions. Some of those questions included:

- Can we expect long-term commitments from faculty if we don't reciprocate?

- How will three-year contracts affect the morale of our tenured and tenure-track faculty who discover they can no longer teach summer school [for an extra wage]?

- Given the rationale of providing strong economic incentives for choosing a three-year appointment, what data are available to suggest the economic incentives in fact will attract the very best faculty? In the context of this proposal, how is "best faculty" being defined?

- Will the productive tenured faculty, who are receiving approximately 3 percent annual raises, continue to put forth such effort when new faculty fresh out of school, who haven't proven themselves, are receiving much more money?

- Will the same standards and criteria for promotion and performance evaluation be used for new-contract faculty as well as for tenure-track faculty? What will be the expectations for professional involvement? How will they demonstrate their achievements?

According to the report's authors, most of the 123 questions remain unanswered.

Several faculty members expressed frustration with the manner in which the administration presented and implemented Policy 302. One tenured faculty member complained, "I'm unaware of *any* discussion of this policy" before it was imposed. "This was not presented to the faculty as something to discuss. It was handed down," agreed Jerry Manion, a tenured faculty member at UCA for thirty-four years. Manion suspected that Policy 302 was a convenient way for "Thompson to implement year-round contracts, which is something he has wanted to do for a while." Bob Willenbrink expressed similar cynicism. "This policy is a way to control faculty," he said. "It's a way to take the decision-making power outside of the faculty and put it in the hands of the people who write the checks."

Even with the undercurrents of confusion and frustration, most faculty members saw no point in overtly protesting the new policy. Many firmly believed that protesting any of President Thompson's decisions would be futile. One tenured faculty member explained: "There's apathy here because for years and years we've had no voice. We're used to a dictatorial regime. . . . We voted no confidence in the president, his contract was extended, and he was given a raise. The president does not listen to any voice. There's mistrust everywhere."

Adlong concurred, saying, "The faculty would say it's futile to try and stop any policy." Provost Mosbo noted that "some faculty feel the president is so powerful that there's no reason to fight his policies."

Others chose not to fight the policy because they were convinced that it would ultimately fail. "I don't think this policy is worth worrying about because I don't think it's workable," Manion commented. Several department chairs gave a simpler explanation for their lack of concern. "I would never recommend this to a recruit," said one. "I would not, as a department chair, ever encourage a faculty member to take a new position under this policy because it leaves no time for independent research or scholarly reflection," said another. "I don't think anyone will take these positions if they understand what they're doing," said a third.

For these department chairs, Policy 302 is largely irrelevant since they, not the president, make the offers to candidates. And if department chairs discourage Policy 302 appointments, or conveniently forget to extend that option, no changes in current departmental hiring practices will occur. With the confidence that change will not occur, these chairs see no need to worry.

Not everyone reacted to the new policy with such relative passivity. In an October 3, 1998, editorial, Michael "William" Link, a resident of Russellville, Arkansas, who was not employed at the institution, wrote: "In my opinion, the remarks of UCA President Winfred Thompson were a farrago of cunning, dissimulation and meretriciousness. . . Setting aside all his jive, I think the UCA plan is a ploy to cover up an ego and power trip, which will destroy tenure, crush academic freedom and make UCA more a factory or a plantation than a university" (Link, 1998, p. B9).

The Policy in Practice

Data from academic year 1998–99, the first year that the policy was in effect, corroborates the department chairs' prediction. The provost reported that "we hired five new tenure-track faculty, each of whom was offered the option of a three-year or tenure-track appointment. . . . There were no faculty who opted for the twelve-month, three-year rolling contracts." For many, the greatest deterrent was the summer teaching requirement. One department chair stated: "For those of us in the sciences, we have great concerns about the obligation of summer teaching. Scientists need a significant amount of time to conduct fieldwork and research, and we simply can't do this if we're required to teach over the summer."

Another tenured faculty member voiced his concerns even more strongly. "A new Ph.D. in the natural sciences would commit professional suicide if he were to accept a twelve-month appointment like this," he said.

This lack of interest among recruits prompted the administration to consider the possibility of a nine-month appointment. The provost commented that such an option "is likely to be added. I am currently working on adapting the policy to include that possibility."[5]

Ambiguity about the original details of the policy presented a second obstacle. Policy 302's stipulations were unclear, as was the question of how substantial the salary premium would actually be. As one chair explained:

> The policy is murky, so it makes it very hard to recruit. We offered a recruit a choice between a tenure-track position on a nine-month contract for a salary of $35,000 or a twelve-month contract under the new policy for $54,900. She took the tenure-track position. Why? Because I had emphasized what the new policy would mean to her. That on a twelve-month contract, she may have to do projects to fill her time that she might not want to do. And while the salary premium seems high, in fact, the monthly gross salary, adjusted for the extra months, is not that different. I felt it was my responsibility to explain to her how tough it would be for her. She'd have no time for professional development. She's only thirty years old.

The "murkiness" even extended to whether the appointments were for "three-year contracts" as one advertisement stated, or for "rolling" contracts that automatically extended contingent upon satisfactory performance.

The budgetary impact of the new policy also raised some concern. Provost Mosbo was uncertain about how the new positions, which would pay a significantly higher wage, would impact the university's budget. While the state allocated thirty of the new positions, it did not provide the university with additional funding. Mosbo commented:

My initial response was that the plan costs money. Will we recover in productivity and effectiveness what we spend financially? We don't yet know. The hope is that the policy will pay off in quality and in research productivity–and that we'll be teaching our students more effectively. But I don't know where the money would come from if ten people accepted these new positions. We'd have to hire fewer faculty. Then we'd have bigger class sections or fewer course offerings. [The money] will come out of my budget, but there's no slack for it right now.

This may become even more of an issue if, as some expect, the president decides to "up the ante" for Policy 302 positions. According to Professor Adlong, if new hires continue to choose traditional appointments over the new contracts, "Thompson said he'll just up the ante and see what price people put on tenure." Provost Mosbo said that while he doesn't "know for sure," he "guesses" the president will raise the salary premium incrementally until someone accepts one of the new appointments.

Other faculty members worried that the new policy could have an adverse effect on collegiality by creating a rift on two fronts: between the tenure-track faculty and new non-tenure-track faculty on the one hand, and between the current non-tenure-track faculty and the new, higher paid "302" faculty on the other. This "two-tier system of non-tenure-track appointees," predicted one professor, was "sure to cause friction within a department."[6] A non-tenure-track instructor in the Department of Speech, Theater, and Mass Communication expressed her fears this way: "I have to teach a huge load, do research on a grant, and do committee work and community service, and I have *no* job security. Not only would faculty members hired under the new policy make significantly more money than me, but they would have the security of two years' notice before their contract could be terminated. Most faculty members with standard non-tenure-track appointments don't know until the last minute whether their contracts will be renewed for the coming academic year.

A relatively new assistant professor of philosophy and religion who had just accepted "a more attractive offer elsewhere," commented: "The talk is that people who take [these new positions] won't be committed to the university because the university isn't committed to them. . . . They're mercenaries, going out to the highest bidder. If your philosophy of a university is that it's a community, you don't want a policy like this. [This policy] pays people for their lack of loyalty."

Despite these various reservations, the silence on campus was louder than any simmering frustration. When asked to characterize the faculty's general reaction to the new policy, President Thompson responded, "Frankly, I thought there'd be more of a negative reaction than there's been."

A Side Rail to the Tenure Track

For academic year 1998–99, the provost recommended nine of twelve candidates for tenure. Two of the three faculty members not endorsed by the provost, but recommended by their departmental committees, petitioned the Faculty Appeals Committee which determined that in both cases the reasons for denial of tenure were "arbitrary and capricious" and that the provost's recommendations should be overturned.

In a seven-page, single-spaced letter to the two individuals and the Appeals Committee, the president made these points: Both "established lackluster but not markedly unsatisfactory records." Their teaching was not "unacceptably inferior" and the research productivity was "limited," but there was nothing in the record to suggest that they were "incapable of meeting" the university's expectations. The rigidities of the tenure system did not allow an extension or a second chance, "even if they markedly improve their teaching and research activities in their terminal year."

Given the essentially permanent nature of tenured appointments, the provost has "a strong disincentive to tenure a faculty member thought to be marginal, even if the individual's personal potential for improvement is acknowledged."

The provost's decisions were rationally based and amply documented. The determination by the Appeals Committee that the decisions were "arbitrary and capricious seems to me egregiously misinformed, misguided, and blatantly biased in favor of the appellants."

The balance of the letter was a strong indictment of tenure. Thompson contended that tenure poses severe disadvantages to both faculty and the institution overall. Anyone familiar with the president's position or his readiness to recite his views was hardly astounded by the criticism of tenure. Yet, as had been the case before, Thompson did have a surprise for everyone. The final page of the letter stated: "In years past, my decision that the recommendations of the provost were not arbitrary and capricious would have fairly conclusively concluded the careers (of these two individuals) at UCA. . . . However, by virtue of Board of Trustees' Policy No. 302, recently adopted, there is an alternative. . . . Although that policy was drafted and adopted with a view of recruitment of new faculty members, it is not by its terms so restricted."

Thompson thereby directed the provost to offer both faculty members a 302 appointment that "provides them with quite generous terms and the opportunity to improve upon their records at the university." They could either accept this offer or serve the final year of a terminal contract. Both accepted rolling contracts and were welcomed back to their departments, although this was somewhat awkward for the one chair who had recommended against tenure for the candidate from his department. The provost said, "I do not know whether or not additional faculty who do not receive tenure will be offered these contracts. There may well be circumstances for which that approach makes good sense, but, in general, I have concerns about doing so."

Creating a Charter University

In many respects, Thompson's efforts to provide alternatives to tenure were secondary to a much larger goal: the reform of higher education or, at the least, the reinvention of UCA as a new model of American higher education. In a glossy publication commemorating his first ten years in office, Thompson answered a self-posed question: "What is my vision for the University of Central Arkansas?"

> I aspire to help build a university where we honor learning in our lives as well as by our professions, where art hits our souls, not merely our ears and eyes, where science and philosophy are not secrets of the gods but familiar tools, kept within easy reach. I hope for a university which not merely trains people to relieve pain or fight ignorance but cultivates the appreciation of beauty in those who otherwise might have been denied its pleasure; a university which motivates its graduates not to ply their trades but to use them to make the world more just and beautiful. My university is respected for the craftsmanship and dedication as well as the intellect of its faculty. It is known for the quality which pervades it, not a reputation which cloaks it; for the prowess of its graduates more than for the preparation of its freshmen.
>
> It reaches up for goals which have not been sought before. It reaches out to students who do not even know those goals exist. It recognizes the nobility of its role in serving the poorly prepared and the impoverished as well as the privileged and the polished. It is honored by alumni for the doors it opened for them; it is respected by faculty for the environment it provides for their creativity; it is supported by the community because its contributions to society are apparent to all.

It may be incongruent with your most cherished sus-
picions of administrators to accept this, but I try not only
to remember but to serve these ideals when I am hag-
gling with the legislature over money, the faculty senate
over athletics, or students over parking lots. . . .I have
discovered that as I grow older, life becomes more pro-
found. The horses' heads have not yet turned so directly
toward that eternity that I can discern whether this pro-
fundity is illuminated because my perception is clearer
or merely because the horizon is closer. In any event, the
less time I have, the more impatient I become with it.
Let us get on with the most enviable task of improving
what is already a very good university.

Through informal conversations with prominent citizens, edu-
cators, legislators, and philanthropists, Thompson decided that this
vision could not be enacted by conducting business as usual. It was
time, he concluded, for revolution, and thus was born a vision of an
institution temporarily called Premier Public University (PPU),
which would, in effect, be a reconstitution of the University of Central Arkansas as a "charter university." PPU would enrich the state's
citizenry with a university of unprecedented stature and preeminent
prestige. PPU would brighten the image of Arkansas nationwide
and catalyze the region's economy.

PPU would be characterized by:

- A highly competitive environment with students
  (future leaders) representative of the racial, economic,
  and ethnic diversity of the state and the union

- Moderate size: 6,000 undergraduate and 1,000 graduate
  students

- Residence on campus for the first two years in order to
  integrate cultural, social, and academic opportunities
  in residential colleges with faculty affiliates

- A curricular emphasis on written and oral communication skills, analytical and quantitative skills, depth in at least one discipline, breadth across several, and knowledge of emerging technologies facilitated by providing every student with a computer upon enrollment

- Thematic general education topics where, for example, "the entire campus might study Asian economy in a given semester"

- Extensive use of one-on-one and small group instruction with faculty teamed with students to form mentor groups which will be the primary vehicle for general education

- A required one-term intramural or extramural experience related to one's major where students apply principles learned

- Required proficiency in at least one language other than English

In Thompson's mind, taking PPU from a dream to reality required two vital ingredients: a substantial infusion of capital and a large measure of institutional autonomy. The first requirement seems possible. An anonymous donor, courted by Thompson over the years and inspired by the president's vision, may consider donating $100 million as an endowment for Premier Public University, if the university will commit to raise an additional $50 million over ten years. Other provisions of the offer include: (1) PPU must operate unencumbered by state intervention, bureaucratic regulation, and partisan politics; (2) the endowment principal would remain under the control of the donor's representatives (such as the foundation trustees) with the income flow committed to the university. The first stipulation reflects the strong conviction of Thompson and the potential donor that PPU can only become truly innovative and distinctive as an essentially private institution. Freedom from state control is, from the potential donor's perspective, nonnegotiable. The second provision reflects this individual's concern that the state could, by subsequent acts, redirect the endowment toward other state programs or priorities. Indeed, "provisions of the agreement will ensure that the commitment of income will cease in the very unlikely event that the state does not fulfill its responsibilities."

Emboldened by the magnitude of the prospective possible gift and hopes for legislative support, Thompson and a small group of senior staff and outside advisers drafted and planned to present to the governor a bill to convert UCA into a "charter university." The formal title of the proposed legislation is "An act to abolish the University of Central Arkansas and to establish a charter university known as Premier Public University." PPU would "operate essentially as a private entity" and "shall not be considered a . . . state agency for the purpose of state statutes and constitutional provisions." This latitude would easily extend, of course, to the abolition of tenure.

In return for the income from a $100 million endowment, the state would commit to sharing operating and capital funds with PPU based on the same per capita allocation as the University of Arkansas at Fayetteville, the state's flagship campus. At present, UCA receives $40 million a year from the state. The state would also have the right to audit all university accounts and the university would operate under the state's freedom of information laws.

The draft legislation proposed that PPU be governed by a board of seven members appointed by the governor for seven-year terms with the advice and consent of the senate, although the initial board would consist of the current UCA board members until each trustee's term expired. The board would be "charged with the management and control of Premier Public University, including determining policies for the organization, administration, and development of the university." The pros and cons of appointing a representative of the potential donor's foundation to the university board has been considered, but not resolved.

The concept of Premier Public University appears to be very much alive. President Thompson plans to work with the governor and other state officials to develop support for his idea. On campus, there are probably more questions than answers, and the number one question may be, "Is Thompson about to pull the biggest rabbit yet out of his hat and, if so, is that a good thing?"

References

Link, Michael "William." (1998). Editorial. *Arkansas Democrat-Gazette*, October 3, p. B9.

Magner, Denise. (1998). "Tenure Will Be Harder to Get, Experts Say, But It Won't Disappear." *Chronicle of Higher Education*, October 23, p. A14.

Zernike, Kate. (1999). "Ark. College's Options Enter Tenure Debate." *Boston Globe*, March 18, p. A1.

Endnotes

1. According to Provost John Mosbo, assistant professors at UCA earned an average salary of $40,800 in 1998–1999. The average national salary for assistant professors during the 1998–1999 academic year was $43,485 as reported by the College and University Personnel Administration (CUPA).

2. Because non-tenure-track faculty members didn't have standard voting privileges at the time, they convened separately and expressed support of the president. According to Lorna Strong, the board officially recognized this body in 1998 as the Non-tenure-track Faculty Senate.

3. Contrary to what was reported in the *Boston Globe*, the premium would not typically be as high as 50 percent.

4. University of Central Arkansas Board Policy #302, "Non-Tenure Track Multi-Year Appointments Policy," March 1999.

5. According to Provost Mosbo, the administration has since approved the use of nine-month appointments under the new policy. The new nine-month salaries will be the national average by rank and discipline. The amount of the premium will be roughly ten to fifteen percent.

6. Contractual arrangements for lecturers, clinical instructors, and lab instructors have since been amended. After four years of service, they may also be placed on three-year rolling contracts.

Discussion Questions

1. Did President Thompson orchestrate an effective organizational change process as he developed Policy 302? Why or why not?

2. Is Policy 302 good for UCA? Why or why not?

3. What are the implications for faculty at UCA if new faculty begin to accept faculty employment under Policy 302? What are the implications of offering Policy 302 non-tenure-track appointments to UCA faculty who do not receive tenure?

4. Does the proposal to transform UCA into Premier Public University represent a threat or an opportunity?

Recommended Background Readings

Berdhal, Robert O., and Terrence J. MacTaggart. (2000). *Charter Colleges: Balancing Freedom and Accountability.* Boston, MA: Pioneer Institute for Public Policy Research.

Chait, Richard. (1994). "Make Us an Offer: Creating Incentives for Faculty to Forsake Tenure." *Trusteeship*, 2(1): 28–29.

Chait, Richard, and C. Ann Trower. (1998). "Build It and Who Will Come? Florida Gulf Coast University Creates a Faculty Without Tenure." *Change*, 30(5): 21–29.

Lataif, Louis. (1998). "A Realistic Alternative to Traditional Tenure." *Chronicle of Higher Education*, June 26, p. B6.

Magner, Denise K. (2000). "The Right Conditions May Lure Scholars Off the Tenure Track, Study Finds." *Chronicle of Higher Education*, March 31.

"More Money Isn't Enough to Forsake Tenure, Massachusetts Profs Say." (1999). *Wall Street Journal*, May 25, p. A1.

O'Neill, James M. (2000). "Tenure May Be Less Vital to New Faculty." *Philadelphia Inquirer*, March 31.

Trower, Cathy A. (1999). "The Trouble With Tenure." *National Forum*, 79(1): 24–29.

6

University of Minnesota
The Politics of Tenure Reform

Cathy A. Trower

"**M**innesota Faculty, Regents Put Tenure to the Test," proclaimed a front page headline of the *Washington Post* article on November 9, 1996. The article highlighted two fundamental questions regarding the place of tenure at the University of Minnesota: (1) To what extent is academic freedom essential to the core values of a university? and (2) What are the implications of eliminating tenure at the University of Minnesota?

To the astonishment of the university's board of regents (BOR), discussions about possible reforms of the university's tenure code had become a "cause celebre." The local, national, and professional press featured the story almost daily, and the Internet was swamped with expressions of concern and outrage from academics across the United States and beyond. Visits to a special Worldwide Web home page devoted to the issue mushroomed. The University of Minnesota was suddenly the flash point for a national debate about the

---

Cathy A. Trower prepared this case as the basis for class discussion rather than to illustrate either effective or ineffective handling of an administrative situation. The information in this case was drawn from the public record.

future of academic tenure. "How," the regents wondered, "did we ever get to this point?"

The University of Minnesota

One of America's largest and most distinguished universities, the "U of M" has more than 200 departments, 60,000 students, and about 3,500 full-time faculty (2,588 or 74 percent tenured and 508 or 14 percent tenure-track). In addition to the Twin Cities campus, where 77 percent of the students and 84 percent of the faculty are located, there are three satellite campuses in Morris, Crookston, and Duluth. (A fourth campus, Waseca, closed in 1991, and the faculty were reassigned to the other sites.)

The Board of Regents' Members and Procedure

The university's board of regents (BOR) has twelve members. Prospective members are screened and interviewed by the Regent Candidate Advisory Council, a committee jointly appointed by the governor, the speaker of the house, and the president of the senate. The council recommends a slate of candidates to the state legislature members, who then vote for their candidates of choice. Regents serve six-year terms subject to reappointment by the legislature. This system has been cited regularly as a national model for trustee selection.

Among the seven men and five women on the U of M board at the time the tenure controversy began were: a former governor, a former school teacher, a student representative, and a labor leader. Three of these twelve members were in their second term. The chairman of the board, Thomas R. Reagan, was initially appointed by the governor in 1991 to fill a vacancy created by a resignation. A former chief of staff for Congressman James Oberstar, Reagan was elected by the legislature to a full term in 1993 and became board chair in 1995.

Nils Hasselmo, a professor of Scandinavian language and literature and academic administrator at Minnesota for almost twenty
years, returned to U of M as president in 1989 after five years away as
provost of the University of Arizona. In 1995, Hasselmo announced
his resignation from the presidency, effective at the end of the
1996–97 academic year. While Hasselmo reported directly to the
board, the regents also had a small, independent staff headed by an
executive director, Steven Bosacker, formerly a congressional aide in
Washington, D.C.

Meetings of the board are conducted in keeping with the state
of Minnesota's "sunshine" law which requires that any board meetings, defined as the assembly of four or more regents, be open to the
public and the press. The law also stipulates that any and all written records, including notes from conversations, are to be regarded
as public documents. Private meetings are allowed only under attor-
ney-client privilege or to discuss labor negotiations.

The Tenure Code Is Put into Play

The board of regents' consideration of changing the tenure code
began on May 11, 1995, when Regent and then Board Chairperson,
Jean Keffeler, a management consultant, "noted that she would like
to review the information available on faculty productivity and
engage in an in-depth discussion about tenure issues, including academic freedom."[1] Keffeler was particularly concerned about the end
to mandatory retirement and the university's capacity to reallocate
resources from low to high program priorities, especially as state
funding for the university had declined 10 percent since 1990. Two
months later, on July 14, 1995, Regent Reagan pledged in his inau-
gural statement, as the new chair of the board, continued attention
to the central issues raised in U-2000, the university's comprehensive strategic plan. Reagan highlighted the need for an enhanced
resource base, affordability, the shifting environment for medical

education, and a backlog of deferred maintenance. In the context of addressing all the challenges that the university faced, Reagan also said that "We may have to make programmatic cuts or take a fresh look at policies such as tenure."

On October 1, 1995, Regent Keffeler received a memorandum from the Office of Human Resources in response to questions she had raised about the governance process to address the issue of tenure. The memorandum explained that the university had a "Tenure Subcommittee of the Senate Committee on Faculty Affairs" which "is a standing committee of the faculty governance system that has been in place since 1985 and is charged with providing advice and recommendations to the Faculty Senate on amendments to, or inter-pretation of, the Tenure Regulations." Under this system, the Tenure Subcommittee would review and advise the Faculty Senate which would, in turn, make final recommendations to the administration. The board of regents would "ultimately approve all modifications to the [Tenure] Regulations." The memo continued, "In 1995–96 this committee has been asked by the senior vice president for academic affairs to review and recommend several modifications to the regu-lations (such as) how to streamline the internal appeal processes associated with denial or termination of tenure."

Concerned that the board did not have a national overview and independent assessment of the issues, the regents invited Dr. Judith Gappa, vice president for human relations at Purdue University, to make a presentation on October 12, 1995. Among other issues, Gappa discussed public skepticism about lifetime employment for faculty with little apparent accountability, public perceptions of a misfit between faculty priorities on the one hand and institutional missions and societal needs on the other hand, and concerns among academics about the "rigidity" of the tenure system. Over the course of the meeting, the regents raised several additional matters: how to remove unproductive faculty, how to measure the performance of tenured and nontenured faculty, and what implications tenure has on the changing role of professors.

The Tenure Review Working Group

After the regents' discussions, Senior Vice President for Faculty Affairs, James Infante, advised the Faculty Consultative Committee (FCC), arguably the most prestigious faculty committee, that tenure was being questioned outside of the university and that "the regents have seen a need to look at it in depth." Although changes may be needed, Infante did not expect tenure to be eliminated. He commented, "I cannot conceive of a more uncompetitive thing to do than do away with tenure."[2]

"To ensure that the faculty and administration were holding the tenure discussions in a coordinated fashion and in cooperation with the regents' schedule, a Faculty-Administration Tenure Review Working Group (TRWG) was established on October 16, 1995, jointly appointed by the senior vice president for academic affairs and the chair of the Faculty Consultative Committee (FCC)."[3] The TRWG was comprised of six members: Professor John Adams, chair of the working group and chair of the Faculty Consultative Committee; Professor Mary Dempsey, chair of the Tenure Subcommittee of the Senate Committee on Faculty Affairs; Daniel Farber, professor of law and acting associate vice president for academic affairs; Carol Carrier, associate vice president for human resources; Paul Quie, regents' professor; and Matthew Tirrell, a department chair.

The President's Perspective

Minutes from an FCC meeting on November 2, 1995, record that President Hasselmo wanted "no misunderstandings about the current [tenure] discussions" and affirmed that "academic freedom is the foundation of universities." However, he continued, "the university must review tenure; that is the best defense for tenure as protection of academic freedom. How tenure comes to be job security must be evaluated, as must the ways tenure is granted and removed and the extent of its application within the university, especially the Medical School."

In a letter to Regent Reagan dated November 20, 1995, Hasselmo delineated what should be examined or reexamined.

> Tenure imposes rigidities and lack of flexibility. There-
> fore, it is important to establish *goals* as to the *proportion*
> of *faculty* in departments that are tenured. It is assumed
> that the proportion of tenured faculty who are tenured
> must decrease. Thus it is important to consider the revi-
> talization and perhaps the *creation of "nontenure" tracks*
> for faculty, and their use in certain areas of the Univer-
> sity. Perhaps tenure should be available only under
> exceptional circumstances in certain areas. . . . *Partial
> decoupling of compensation from tenure* should be examined
> (base salary plus; possibility of decrease in salary). . . . At
> the University of Minnesota tenure is held within the
> institution. At some other universities tenure is held at
> the department level—a more flexible arrangement. The
> *location of tenure* should be reexamined. . . . The *length of
> the probationary period* is seven years, except in the clini-
> cal fields of the Medical School. The length of the proba-
> tionary period should be reexamined. . . . [The university
> should] *clarify* and remove unnecessary bureaucratic pro-
> cedures from the *process* of granting tenure, and carefully
> examine the effectiveness of the present process of post-
> tenure merit review and examine alternatives. The pres-
> ent *processes* of dealing with alleged or proven *misconduct*
> of tenured (and tenure-track) faculty are very complex
> and lengthy. They are open to numerous appeal processes
> before administrative actions can be enforced. In order
> to effectively and appropriately manage the institution,
> we must initiate a process redesign effort to simplify and
> shorten these processes while still protecting the rights
> of the accused.

In a memo dated January 2, 1996, to the chancellors and provosts, Hasselmo stated, "The planning and budget decisions we make must be strategic. By this I mean that we have to shape the future of the institution in making those decisions, to the limit of what is possible at this time, even against considerable and contractual obstacles. This means that we have to target programs and functions for elimination, curtailment, or reorganization, even if there are obstacles having to do with tenure and other contractual obligations."

The Academic Health Center

In December 1995, the regents' interest in the tenure code intensified when William Brody, appointed provost of the Academic Health Center (AHC) by Hasselmo, described for the board the economic crisis that confronted medical education. Brody enumerated major changes in medicine and health care that were placing "particularly strong and somewhat unique stresses on academic health centers across the country." Among these external pressures were:

- Rapid shifts in the funding sources to support undergraduate and graduate medical education and research

- The need to increase the number of primary care physicians who provide the patients to fulfill the center's mission, even though many of these additional doctors may lack the qualifications to be promoted to tenure, or in many cases even appointed to a tenure-track faculty position

- The requirement to integrate educational curricula across traditional disciplines, for example, integrated team teaching of pharmacy, nursing, and medical students

- The need to add new disciplines (public health, administration, and business skills) to the more traditional professional student curricula

Brody stated that "leading universities are beginning to recognize that these extraordinary changes require rethinking the role of tenure in providing long-term viability of their institutions. The University of Minnesota has one of the least flexible systems of tenure, and the fact that other academic medical centers with more flexibility in their tenure codes than ours are considering significant modifications to their tenure systems, should indicate to the regents that their discussions of this issue are both timely and in keeping with the nationwide trend."

Brody stressed that the

> Current tenure system hinders change and the AHC's ability to respond to changes in the demand for its educational, research, and service programs . . . [in that it] limits AHC's ability to manage its largest expense—faculty salaries; limits AHC's ability to prioritize faculty efforts; limits AHC's ability to motivate faculty and ensure faculty productivity; limits AHC's ability to change the composition of the faculty to meet the changing needs of those who use our educational, research, and service programs.

> Management has no ability to deal efficiently and effectively with faculty misconduct: obligations of faculty members under tenure definitions are too vague; [there are] no actions short of detenuring someone for misconduct; [the] grievance/judicial system is prolonged, expensive, and lacks finality; and there is a need for clearer guidelines for promotion and dismissal.

While Brody did not offer any specific proposals, he outlined several possibilities: "a change in the relationship between tenure and compensation; non-tenure-track faculty lines that otherwise carry the same privileges and obligations as tenure-track lines; and changing the rank at which tenure is bestowed." He suggested that four principles should guide considerations of tenure reform: "protection of academic freedom, rewards for performance, efficient means to resolve disputes, and flexibility to adjust to changing demands."

As a direct result of Brody's presentation, the regents adopted a resolution in December 1995 to

> Assure the protection of academic freedom; to provide University decision makers with the flexibility to respond to the institution's changing circumstances, and to shape academic and administrative programs to meet the needs of our teaching, research, and service missions; to ensure the maintenance of a vital academy through ongoing programs of faculty renewal, including effective tools for development and retention; to maintain fairness as a central criterion in personnel decisions; to address the special tenure concerns of the AHC; and to provide the Board with opportunities for public discussion of eventual revisions in the tenure code.

The board directed the "administration to develop policy recommendations for review and action prior to the start of the 1996–97 academic year," and the regents agreed to seek special funding for AHC during the 1996 legislative session.[4]

The State Legislature

In January 1996, the legislature began to hear testimony on the tenure issue. Appearing before the legislature on February 19, 1996, President Hasselmo stated, "In the case of tenured faculty members when we make programmatic changes, we will retain, reassign, and we will provide buyout opportunities if [the faculty] do not choose to go elsewhere when that programmatic change is made. But we are not going to fire tenured faculty members."

The next day, Frank Cerra, dean of the medical school, reaffirmed before the Higher Education Finance Committee of the House the necessity of tenure to protect academic freedom. However, Cerra also declared that change in the current tenure code was "essential" for the university and the AHC, "particularly in such areas as human resources management and productivity-based compensation."

In March 1996, legislation was passed that tied $6.6 million for the AHC to reform of the tenure code. "The legislature requests the faculty, administration, and board of regents of the university to pursue an internal process leading to changes in the tenure code applicable to the Academic Health Center, without infringing on academic freedom." The money would be released only when the board of regents "certifies" that appropriate changes had been made to the tenure code.

On March 7–8, 1996, the BOR discussed initial ideas from the Tenure Review Working Group. The group presented six areas for further consideration:

- A new introduction to the tenure code forcefully explaining the justification for tenure

- Interpretations of the current code that would emphasize its actual, but so far underutilized, flexibility

- Changes to allow the Judicial Committee to more efficiently review appeals of tenure decisions

- Limited additional flexibility for colleges within the university to extend the probationary period

- A policy on post-tenure review to allow constructive intervention when faculty members perform unsatisfactorily over time

- Initiation of a process to redefine the status and rights of "nonregular" faculty (non-tenure-track).[5]

Reactions to Possible Reforms

Concerned that President Hasselmo and the board of regents were "launching a serious campaign to end tenure not only at the university, but nationally as well," faculty formed a union in March 1996.

The University Faculty Alliance (UFA)

In the spring of 1996, an e-mail communiqué announced that "The UFA is now soliciting signatures on authorization statements for collective bargaining representation. If sufficient numbers of signatures are obtained, the union can request a cease and desist order from the state Bureau of Mediation Services to prevent changes in conditions of employment until a collective bargaining representation election is held."

External Protests

Word of the university's "assault" on tenure spread rapidly, most notably by e-mail. In response to the perceived threat to tenure, faculties across the country expressed grave concerns. The Academic Senate of the University of California resolved on April 8, 1996, that the "Regents of the University of Minnesota should cease all efforts to undermine the institution of tenure, whether by easing restrictions on the termination of tenured faculty or by forcing tenured faculty to leave by decoupling their compensation from tenure."

Soon thereafter, the Executive Council of the Rutgers Council of American Association of University Professors (AAUP) chapters resolved that "we strongly protest the efforts of the Regents of the University of Minnesota to undermine the institution of academic tenure by whatever means. We call upon the regents and the president to heed the lessons of history, including that of the University of Minnesota itself, and stand firm against all who would render our institutions of higher learning vulnerable to pressure for ideological conformity of whatever persuasion."

The University Faculty Senate

Locally, the rage was most intense. While most of the anger was directed toward the regents and the administration, there was considerable disappointment with the Tenure Review Working Group. Thus, on April 18, 1996, "the Faculty Senate passed a resolution that had the effect of disbanding the *ad hoc* Tenure Working Group. . . and turning subsequent governance deliberations regarding Tenure Code revision over to three faculty governance committees—the Tenure Subcommittee, the Judicial Committee, and the Senate Committee on Faculty Affairs."[6]

The President's New Perspective

In an effort to quell the heightened anxieties and outrage, and to reassure the community of the university's bedrock commitment to tenure, Hasselmo summarized the "core concepts" that had to be preserved.

- Going forward, the code revision adopted by the university should not disturb the terms of any faculty member's contract.

- Individual faculty members' tenure should continue to be sited at the institutional or systemwide level.

- Individual tenured faculty should not be laid off for any reason other than financial exigency.

He then addressed the areas of change that he believed were "most important to the successful completion of the tenure deliberations."

- To clarify that department heads may assign tasks to faculty members; and that reassignments and retraining may be necessary in the case of program change

- To define the categories of faculty appointment in which tenure may be granted

- To permit colleges to extend the probationary period up to nine years

- To reaffirm that everyone's base salary is guaranteed and that tenure is tied exclusively to base salary and not to other income sources (overload or summer session earnings, administrative stipends, clinical earnings, bonuses and other forms of incentives)

- To develop, in cooperation with the Judicial Committee, more time-efficient and effective judicial processes

- To effect a meaningful post-tenure review process

Additional statements from Hasselmo's office underscored an "iron-clad protection of academic freedom" and suggested that "the tenure code would be changed in ways that would improve its:

1. *Clarity*—by more fully explicating its purposes
2. *Flexibility*—by recognizing the different employment rights, roles, and responsibilities attached to different types of appointments; and by introducing more unit-specific flexibility, such as variable periods of probationary appointments
3. *Faculty and administrative accountability*—by installing systematic post-tenure review processes

4. *Efficiency*—by both formalizing and streamlining Judicial Committee proceedings and revising rules relevant to removal-for-cause actions

These four criteria are crucial to achieving the vision stated in our *University 2000* strategic plan.

Proposed Amendments to the Tenure Code by the Faculty Senate

The Tenure Subcommittee (which, in effect, replaced the Tenure Review Working Group) deliberated throughout the spring of 1996. On May 30 and June 6, the subcommittee presented and the senate approved twelve motions and four interpretations of sections of the tenure code. The most relevant motions and interpretations follow:

Motion B incorporated the current BOR statement on academic freedom into the tenure regulations.

Motion C changed "nonregular" to "term" appointment and tightened the standards for term appointments of clinical faculty. "This [amendment] recognizes the variable funding of such clinical activities and does not commit the university to maintaining the income of future clinicians if the clinical revenues will not support them."

Motion D clarified the relationship between base pay and other temporary compensation.

> Each faculty member shall receive a base salary, which shall not be decreased except as expressly authorized in these regulations. The base salary shall consist of the initial base salary plus any subsequent increase. In general . . . salary increases will be added to the base. The University may also provide a faculty member with additional compensation that is not part of the base salary. The additional compensation may be for special awards or activities in addition to regular faculty responsibilities

such as clinical practice, administrative service, overload duties, summer school teaching, and summer research support. The faculty member does not have a right to continuation of this additional compensation beyond the time for which it is granted.

An interpretive comment stated that "The current base salary of faculty members will be guaranteed under this system."

Motion E permitted the tenured faculty of a college to extend the probationary period to nine years.

Motion F authorized the Judicial Committee to receive independent legal advice from outside counsel, appointed by the committee "in consultation with the president."

Motion G simplified disciplinary proceedings by removing a formal review of the dean's decision by the vice president, and a formal review by the board of regents of the final decision by the president.

Motion H mandated a peer-driven, post-tenure review of faculty and permitted salary reductions for poor performance. The process required that each academic unit establish goals and expectations for all faculty members with respect to teaching, scholarly productivity, service, and outreach. The goals must meet five stipulations: (1) address each area of activity; (2) take into account stages of faculty career development; (3) allow for flexible assignments and differential emphases consistent with the unit's mission; (4) respect each faculty member's academic freedom; and (5) include reasonable indices or measures of performance for each area.

Special reviews would be triggered if and when both the unit head and the Peer Merit Review Committee find a faculty member's performance to be "substantially below goals and expectations of the unit." In such cases, faculty members would be provided specific, written suggestions for improvement and a time period of at least one year for remediation.

If the faculty member remains "substantially below goals and expectations" at the conclusion of the period for improvement, the unit head and the Merit Review Committee "may, with the dean's concurrence, jointly request that a special peer review committee be empanelled to prepare a report on the faculty member's performance." The committee would include four members elected, by secret ballot, by the tenured members of the unit, plus one member appointed by the individual under review. This committee could recommend: (1) that performance is satisfactory; (2) reassignment of duties in light of the faculty member's strengths; (3) specified steps to improve subject to regular annual reviews; (4) specified steps to improve subject to another special review; and (5) limited reductions in salary, with six months' notice, where performance is "so inadequate," not to exceed 10 percent of base salary as a result of any one special review and no more than 25 percent over time.

Motion I formally recognized "outreach activity that extends a faculty member's teaching, research, and service beyond the campus or to nontraditional groups of students" as an appropriate criterion for tenure in light of the university's mission.

Motion J added a preamble to the tenure regulations that characterized tenure as "the keystone to academic freedom" and as "part of a social compact which recognizes that tenure serves important public purposes and benefits society."

Interpretation 1 reaffirmed that "faculty members have the freedom to choose research topics and discuss relevant matters in classes. In addition, faculty members have the responsibility to carry out teaching assignments made by their department head. This interpretation also provides for procedures to be followed when a faculty member considers a teaching assignment to be unreasonable."[7]

Interpretation 2 reiterated that "in case of programmatic change, the university recognizes its obligation to continue the employment of regular faculty." After consultation with the individual, new responsibilities, "as closely related to the original appointment as practicable," may be assigned by a university officer. If assignments in the faculty member's discipline are not feasible, the individual may be required to teach in another field, where qualified, or to perform professional or administrative duties, or to undertake at university expense an educational program to acquire new skills. If a mutually agreeable assignment cannot be made, the faculty member may file a formal grievance. Other voluntary options included early retirement packages, reduced time appointments, and severance agreements.

Hasselmo publicly hailed the senate's proposal. The amendments "squarely address and clearly satisfy" the criteria and objectives the president had previously established. He commended the faculty for their "collective willingness to provide leadership in this area." Further, he wrote, "The faculty, the Executive Council and I are in full agreement on the policies underlying these changes. Individual faculty should not be laid off at the University for any reason other than institutional financial exigency. The Executive Council unanimously supports this position, which is that of the Faculty Senate." With some modest modifications, the president remarked, "the faculty's proposals . . . satisfy the Legislature's condition upon release of its performance incentive account for the AHC."[8]

Reactions to the Senate's Recommendations

The Consultant's Report

In late March 1996, a few months before the senate's action, the BOR issued a "request for proposal" for a consultant to advise the board and to evaluate any recommendations that emerged from the faculty senate. In May, the board selected Richard Chait, a professor at the University of Maryland and the author of several articles and a book on tenure.

In a report submitted on July 2, 1996, the consultant praised the university community for a discussion that was "civil and cordial—much to the credit of the faculty, the administration, and the Board. The proposed amendments, taken together, are progressive and constructive actions." On the other hand, the report noted that the prohibition against layoffs due to program discontinuation provided an "extraordinary measure of employment security," further rein-forced by a guaranteed base salary and the university-wide, rather than departmentally based, locus of tenure. In addition, there were no provisions to terminate programs for qualitative reasons and lim-ited incentive to do so for financial reasons as "little money will be harvested for reallocation from any program closure that does not recapture the dollars attached to faculty salaries."

If the regents should decide to change current policies on pro-gram discontinuation, the locus of tenure, or salary guarantees, the report continued, "faculty leaders believe that the goodwill of many peers will evaporate and that a movement to unionize will acceler-ate. These are not trivial costs." The consultant urged the board to focus more on policy objectives and intended results. "At the moment, I believe there may be too much focus on policy formula-tion and too little on policy *objectives*. Once the objectives are delin-eated, the University can consider multiple pathways to the intended results."

Elected Officials

On June 7, 1996, State Representative Becky Kelso commented on public radio that the senate's proposed changes were enough to meet the letter of the law but that the recommendations did not go far enough, particularly in the area of faculty layoffs. Likewise, the governor's chief of staff reported that the governor felt that the pro-posed changes to the tenure code needed to go further.[9]

In a letter to Regent Reagan dated July 2, 1996, Laura King, State Commissioner of Finance, declared that "there is ample evi-dence that both the letter and the spirit of the legislative language is unmet by [the faculty's] proposal. Adoption of the senate proposal, without substantial revisions, is an inadequate response to legisla-tive expectations. If no action is taken, the release of the funds may be jeopardized." King recommended that the "board delay consid-eration until the issue of legislative compliance is adequately addressed."

On July 11, 1996, Regent Reagan received a letter from Representative Kelso which claimed that the faculty recommendations fell short in three respects. First, the faculty recommendations do not provide a clear link between performance and compensation." Second, "the faculty recommendations do not allow university leadership the flexibility to respond to evolving programmatic needs. The tenure code should not be a constraint as the University makes the necessary adjustments to a changing environment." And third, the proposed changes "make the post-tenure review process (as well as the grievance process) so complex and cumbersome that it is virtually unworkable. . . . Without effective tenure reform, it will be difficult if not impossible for the University to achieve the goals of U-2000."

The Search for Consensus

At this stage, there appeared to be substantial agreement among the faculty, the president, and the board about many of the tenure code revisions suggested by the senate. Indeed, Regent Keffeler, widely regarded as the most "hard-nosed" and "business-like" board member, recommended that the BOR "approve and adopt outright seven of the twelve motions," including the motions on academic freedom and extended probationary periods. Keffeler proposed that three other motions be accepted in principle but returned to the senate for further clarification and elaboration, and an independent analysis of best practices elsewhere. These three areas were: appeals processes for contested tenure decisions and sanctions for disciplinary actions; post-tenure review; and recognition of "outreach" as a criterion for tenure. The board would defer outright two other motions: guarantees of base salary and appointment of a legal officer for the Judicial Committee. Deferral was also recommended for Interpretation 2, the proscription against layoffs due to program discontinuation.

In order to consider the senate's proposals in depth, the BOR had an off-campus retreat at a lakeside resort in northern Minnesota.

Open to the public and the press, attendees included a dozen or so faculty leaders invited by the board, the regents' outside legal counsel from Hogan & Hartson in Washington, D.C., and Professor Chait. The retreat centered around the four most problematic areas: a guaranteed base salary, program discontinuation, post-tenure review, and the adjudication process. No decisions were to be made at the retreat; the purpose was dialogue and discussion, and the conversations were spirited but cordial.

The faculty was especially vocal on the issue of guaranteed base pay and, even more so, on the prohibition against program-based layoffs. Faculty leaders contended that a change in policy would destroy the "social compact" between the university and the professors, and jeopardize Minnesota's ability to recruit the very best faculty. Layoff authority was unneeded because retirements (an estimated 370 over the next decade) and normal attrition (historically about 5 percent annually) would provide ample flexibility. Furthermore, the *absence* of a layoff provision was what allowed the university to close the Waseca campus, a major reorganization that other institutions would have found impossible.[10] Any erosion of university-wide tenure would be tantamount to a layoff provision because, as Law Professor Fred Morrison, a key draftsman of the senate's proposal, explained, "To convert that guarantee into one supported only by the head of the unit and by the department's resources would communicate a lack of university support to every faculty member and instill in all of us a sense of insecurity."

The Regents' Revised Tenure Code

After the retreat, the regents directed Hogan & Hartson to produce a document that codified the areas of agreement between the faculty and the board, and that proposed policy language broadly reflective of the board's viewpoint on matters where consensus had not yet been reached with the faculty. Prior to the retreat, the attorneys had conferred privately with nearly every regent in order to better understand each individual's concerns and to determine the range of opinions among board members. Hogan & Hartson believed that the regents wanted to be responsible fiduciaries and prudent guardians of the university's long-term welfare, roles that would require policy changes.

As Regent Reagan and others repeatedly stated, the Hogan & Hartson codification, which was presented to the regents on September 3, 1996, was a draft document. After reading the draft, Hasselmo urged the regents, in a "passionate letter," not to consider the document. "The proposed draft will harm the university. It will also rupture cooperative relationships with the faculty for the foreseeable future and perhaps change university governance as we know it."

With respect to the two most contested issues, the key provisions of the regents' draft were as follows:

Salary Guarantees

"Each faculty member shall receive a base salary. Absent reasons found to be compelling by the Board of Regents or its delegate, it is expected that a faculty member's base salary will not be decreased" except under fiscal emergency, or as a sanction as provided in the new post-tenure review policy.

Programmatic Change

At least 60 days before the University discontinues or restructures any program in a way that may lead to the termination of regular faculty appointments before their ordinary expiration, the president shall provide the Board of Regents with a report which describes the proposed action, the educational considerations, or other reasons that support the proposed action, the manner in which the proposed action fits within the long-term policy and planning of the university, and the faculty appointments that would likely be affected by the action. The report shall also describe the University's plans and guidelines for offering reassignment, retraining, and other benefits.

Reassignment and retraining of displaced faculty would be provided "to the extent practicable." If these options were not practicable in the university's judgment "within a reasonable period, were not successful, or were rejected by the faculty member," then the university could terminate the individual.

Daniel Farber and Fred Morrison each analyzed the Hogan & Hartson draft for the benefit of the administration and the faculty senate, respectively.[11]

Base Salary

"Under the [regents'] proposal," Farber asserted, "base pay will no longer represent a clear commitment on the part of the University" because of clauses such as "it is expected that" and "absent compelling reasons." Morrison charged that the changes would "effectively remove all protection of base pay."

Program Discontinuation

"Any change in the University's curriculum or priorities," Farber commented, "could potentially lead to the termination of faculty. Restrictions on this power are either vague and undefined, or else subject to the sole discretion of the University." Morrison concurred.

> The draft appears to exclude faculty from the development of academic policy and plans. This is a deviation from our tradition of "shared governance." [The draft] ignores the expertise of faculty. This transforms the protection of tenure into a protection only so long as the President and Regents continue the faculty member's program. . . . The draft does not firmly commit the University to offer reemployment or retraining. Thus, the probability of finding a suitable place for a terminated fac-

ulty member is lower under this policy than under that
offered by the Faculty Senate's interpretation. Under this
proposal, it would be easier to dismiss a faculty member
if there were no financial crisis, than if there were one!

Furthermore, the draft introduced "restructuring," a vague, objec-
tionable, corporate concept, as a trigger for layoffs.

To make matters worse, the faculty was especially offended by
several provisions that had never been broached before and that
seemed far beyond the scope of the initial discussions. Taken together, these additions constituted for the faculty a breach of faith,
a rupture of the governance process, and a shift from shared governance to legal risk management. Among the most flagrant provisions
from the faculty's perspective were disciplinary action, the post-
tenure review process, and the adjudication process and Judicial
Committee.

Disciplinary Action

New language seemingly required that faculty "maintain standards
of competence and a proper attitude of industry and cooperation
with others within and without the university community. If an
environment of intellectual integrity and mutual respect is to be
maintained, it is necessary to take disciplinary action when commonly held standards of conduct are violated."[12]

"The basis for discharging a tenured faculty member has been
broadened," wrote Farber. The regents' proposal for faculty discipline is "vague and capable of great abuse," Morrison remarked.
"With all due respect, this seems more reminiscent of elementary
school teachers' contracts of the 1920s than of the standards for a
great university. This language seems designed to suppress controversy or dissent." It "would exercise a chilling effect on intellectual
inquiry" because of its "vagueness."

The proposed code also added "adequate cause" and "other
grave misconduct" as reasons for termination or suspension, which

heretofore were limited to *sustained* refusal to perform assigned duties, unprofessional conduct, egregious or *repeated* misuse of power, or sexual harassment. The new version deleted the qualifiers "sustained" refusal and "egregious or repeated" misuse of power. "The removal of 'sustained' . . . and 'egregious or repeated'," Morrison contended, "would make single instances of refusal to perform duties (or misuse of position) punishable by dismissal, even if they were not egregious."

Finally, the revised code permitted administrators to reduce base salaries temporarily or permanently as a "lesser sanction" for disciplinary purposes, subject to advance notice and the opportunity to respond, but without "formal proceedings of any kind." The faculty member could, however, file a grievance after the fact.

Post-Tenure Review Process

The new draft shifted overall responsibility for the design and implementation of the process from departments to colleges, and specified that the annual review would be conducted by the department head, not by faculty peers. For substandard performers, each unit would devise an intensive peer review process "consistent with the principles of peer evaluation." The possible consequences of negative reviews included a 10 percent annual reduction, but omitted were the 25 percent cap as well as the possibility that salary cuts could be entirely restored contingent upon improved performance.

Farber believed that the new language "provides less protection to the faculty than any previous proposal" because "unlike the senate proposal, there is no explicit provision regarding faculty control of the review." Morrison warned that the proposal "shifts responsibility for developing goals and expectations from the department level to the collegiate level." Furthermore, the regents' plan: "repeatedly emphasizes the availability of . . . severe options" for faculty discipline; "eliminates the concept of peer review from the annual review process"; lacks consistency because it "allows each college to establish its own procedures"; and "sets a tone that the entire process is aimed not at improving performance, but at firing people." "The regents' proposal," Morrison concluded, "essentially changed the document from a 'human resources' model . . . to a 'disciplinary model' . . . an unenlightened and vindictive approach."

The Adjudication Process and Judicial Committee

The new draft required the president's "approval" of the Judicial Committee's legal officer; previous language required "consultation" with the president. The committee's rules would be subject to "review and approval" by the regents. Whereas current policy required that the president "shall not" take action materially different from the committee's recommendation without prior consultation, now the president "*may* meet or otherwise consult with the committee" before taking action.

In Farber's estimation, (1) "The Judicial Committee will lose control over its own proceedings"; (2) "The committee's decisions will receive less deference"; and (3) "Administrators will gain the power to punish faculty members severely without any prior review of the decision." According to Morrison, the regents' proposal would permit the president to deviate from the recommendations of the panel that heard the case "for any reason, however trivial," instead of only for "compelling reasons," and would allow the president "to act secretly."

Faculty Furor

The regents' draft inflamed the faculty and produced a firestorm of negative reactions. "It is clear from these proposals," Morrison declared, "that the regents who are promoting them have no respect for the faculty." A leader of the University Faculty Alliance condemned the draft as "far more extreme than anyone believed the regents would advance. . . . They are not really interested in faculty feedback." Even more dramatically, a professor of engineering likened the situation to the Holocaust. "The regents managed to round up the faculty, we are at the train station, and the doors of the boxcars have been locked." Keffeler's suggestion to defer action on the most controversial items was no more than "backing the train out of sight for a few years until we get a conductor—a new president—who will be more cooperative."

In a torrent of letters to the editors of local newspapers, faculty characterized the regents' proposal as an "insult to the faculty," "a new McCarthyism of corporate reengineering," "an all-out assault on academic freedom," "a betrayal," and "treachery." Even Hasselmo openly parted company with the board. "With what seems solid opposition by faculty and solid opposition from the administration, I cannot believe it's in the interests of the institution to impose these requirements." Martin Michaelson, lead counsel from Hogan & Hartson, "disputed that assessment. It's always possible to conjure up a parade of horrible outcomes. But the board's proposal does not warrant that. The proposal is a moderate one, consistent with the approach taken by many universities." Under the present code, he opined, "governance is tilted toward faculty control to an extent that is out of line with most institutions" (Magner, 1996).

Editorial reaction was mixed. The *St. Paul Pioneer Press* (October 2, 1996) called on faculty and regents to "pursue compromise." However, the editors warned that the "university would be harmed if the regents were to capitulate to pressure that they withdraw their recent tenure proposal in its entirety. A humiliation of the regents would destroy the credibility of the board as the governing body of the university." The *Star Tribune* (September 24, 1996) urged the regents to "indicate their willingness to withdraw their proposal to permit layoffs when academic programs are restructured. They should say yes to the more temperate changes the faculty proposed in June." The *Rochester Post Bulletin* (September 11, 1996) described tenure as "anachronistic in today's fast-moving business and professional world" but criticized the board's failure to justify the changes as part of a specific plan to achieve strategic goals. "Fundamental change is needed at the university. A revised tenure policy may be needed to carry out that change. But it is not likely to be changed successfully unless the regents can justify it in terms of an overall reform of university operations." The *Duluth News-Tribune* (November 4, 1996) argued that the faculty were "in the wrong fight." The "enemy was state finances, not hostile regents."

The furor over the board's proposal captured national attention. It was *the* story in higher education; even the *Washington Post* dispatched a reporter to investigate the situation. Against that backdrop, a professor of education on the Duluth campus wrote in a monthly column for the local *Duluth News-Tribune* (Bowman, 1996) under the headline "Nation Watching U's Tenure Battle" that "The educational eyes of the United States are on the University of Minnesota." With everyone watching, the regents pondered what to do. Meanwhile, the University Faculty Alliance gathered strength, momentum, and perhaps, most importantly, signatures for a union election.

References

Bowman, Tom. "Nation Watching U's Tenure Battle."(1996). *Duluth News-Tribune*, September 22.

"Faculty, Regents Need to Pursue Compromise." (1996). (Editorial.) *St. Paul Pioneer Press*, October 2.

Magner, Denise. (1996). "Minnesota Regents' Proposals Would Effectively Abolish Tenure, Faculty Leaders Say." *Chronicle of Higher Education*, September 20, p. A10–A11.

Sanchez, Rene. (1996). "Minnesota Faculty, Regents Put Tenure to the Test." *Washington Post*, November 9, p. A1.

"'U' and Tenure." (1996). (Editorial.) *Star Tribune*, September 24.

"'U' Faces Crisis Over Tenure." (1996). (Editorial.) *Rochester Post Bulletin*, September 11.

"UM Faculty in Wrong Fight." (1996). (Editorial.) *Duluth News-Tribune*, November 4.

Endnotes

1. From the Board of Regents, Faculty, Staff, and Student Affairs Committee minutes, May 11, 1995.

2. University of Minnesota, *Brief*, Vol. XXV, No. 34, October 25, 1995. Editor: Maureen Smith.

3. Memorandum dated April, 18, 1996, from President Nils Hasselmo to members of the university senate.

4. Brody subsequently retained CSC Index, the Cambridge, Massachusetts, firm that pioneered "reengineering" in the corporate sector, to assist the Health Center. CSC's approach and recommendations were widely viewed by the faculty as inappropriate, excessively severe, and far too business-oriented.

5. Materials from the March 7–8, 1996, board meeting, "Concrete Proposals for Tenure Reform: An Agenda for Discussion."

6. Letter dated April 18, 1996, from Nils Hasselmo to the board of regents and attached letter to the university senate.

7. Letter dated June 7, 1996, from Mary Dempsey (Chair, Tenure Subcommittee and Senate Committee on Faculty Affairs) to Ettore Infante (Senior Vice President for Academic Affairs).

8. Memorandum dated June 11, 1996, from President Hasselmo to the board of regents and the Faculty Consultative Committee.

9. Memorandum dated June 7, 1996, from Kim Isenberg (regents' staff) to the board of regents.

10. When the Waseca campus was closed, thirteen faculty accepted retirement packages, and twenty were reassigned, some to positions "created for the sake of reassignment."

11. Farber analysis dated September 2, 1996, entitled "The Consultants' Tenure Proposal: A Preliminary Analysis"; Morrison analysis dated September 10, 1996, entitled "Analysis of Regents' Tenure Proposals."

12. Legal counsel noted that this language was adopted virtually verbatim from a similar policy from the Michigan State faculty handbook.

Discussion Questions

1. What led the board of regents to conclude that they should examine the tenure code at the University of Minnesota?

2. Were the regents' concerns warranted? Why or why not?

3. What role should a board play in decisions concerning reform of the tenure code, or program closure and curriculum? What does shared governance look like in practice?

4. Was a fight with the faculty inevitable? If so, was it a fight that had to be fought with the regents?

5. Was there a win/win policy scenario in this case?

6. Who gained what in the end?

Recommended Background Readings

Birnbaum, Robert. (1988). "Problems of Governance, Management, and Leadership in Academic Institutions." In *How Colleges Work*, (pp. 3–29). San Francisco: Jossey-Bass.

Chait, Richard P. (1997). "Thawing the Cold War Over Tenure." *Trusteeship*, 5(9): 11–15.

Chait, Richard P. (2000). "Trustees and Professors: So Often at Odds, So Much Alike." *Chronicle of Higher Education*, August 4, p. B4.

Engstrand, Gary. (1998). "The Tenure Wars: The Battles and the Lessons." *American Behavioral Scientist*, 41(5): 607–626.

Farber, Daniel A. (1997). "The Miasma in Minnesota." *Trusteeship*, 5(3): 6–10.

Morrison, Fred L. (September 1997). "Tenure Wars: An Account of the Controversy at Minnesota." *Journal of Legal Education*, 47(3): 369–391.

Perley, James E. (1997). "Faculty and Governing Boards: Building Bridges." *Academe*, 83(5): 34–37.

"The Struggle for Tenure Reform." *Minnesota Daily Online*. Available: www.daily.umn.edu/library/focus/tenure.html

Trower, Cathy A., and James P. Honan. (2002). "How Might Data Be Used?" In Richard P. Chait, ed., *The Questions of Tenure*. Cambridge, MA: Harvard University Press.

Selected Bibliography on the Academic Profession and Organizational Change

Literature on the Academic Profession

Bennett, John B., and Shirley S. Chater. (Spring 1984). "Evaluating the Performance of Tenured Faculty Members." *Educational Record*, 65(2): 38–41.

Boyer, Ernest. (1990). *Scholarship Reconsidered: Priorities of the Professoriate*. New Jersey: The Carnegie Foundation for the Advancement of Teaching.

Chait, Richard, and Cathy A. Trower. (1997). *Where Tenure Does Not Reign: Colleges with Contract Systems*. New Pathways Working Paper Series, Inquiry #3. Washington, D.C.: American Association for Higher Education.

Finkelstein, Martin J., Robert K. Seal, and Jack H. Schuster. (1998). *The New Academic Generation: A Profession in Transformation*. Baltimore, MD: The Johns Hopkins University Press.

Furniss, W. Todd. (1977). "Academic Tenure." In Asa Knowles, ed., *International Encyclopedia of Higher Education*. San Francisco: Jossey-Bass.

Goodman, Madeleine J. (1994). "The Review of Tenured Faculty at a Research University: Outcomes and Appraisals." *Review of Higher Education*, 18(1): 83–94.

Hansen, W. L. (1988). "Merit Pay in Higher Education." In D.W. Breneman and Ted I. K. Youn, eds., *Academic Labor Markets and Careers*, pp. 114–137. New York: Falmer Press.

Kasten, K. L. (1984). "Tenure and Merit Pay as Rewards for Research, Teaching, and Service at a Research University." *Journal of Higher Education*, 55: 500–514.

Lewis, Lionel S. (1980). "Academic Tenure: Its Recipients and Its Effects." *Annals of the American Academy of Political and Social Science*, 448: 86–101.

Massy, William F., and Andrea K. Wilger. (1995). "Improving Faculty Productivity: What Faculty Think About It, and Its Effect on Quality." *Change, 27* (July/August 1995): 10–20.

McPherson, Michael S., and Morton Owen Schapiro. (Winter 1999). "Tenure Issues in Higher Education." *Journal of Economic Perspectives, 13*(1): 85–98.

McPherson, Michael S., and Gordon Winston. (1988). "The Economics of Academic Tenure: A Relational Perspective." In David Breneman and Ted I. K. Youn, eds., *Academic Labor Markets and Careers,* pp. 174–199. New York: Falmer Press.

Miller, R. I. (1987). *Evaluating Faculty for Promotion and Tenure.* San Francisco: Jossey-Bass.

O'Toole, James, William W. Van Alstyne, and Richard P. Chait. (1979). *Three Views: Tenure.* New York: Change Magazine Press.

Tierney, William G. (1998). "Tenure Matters: Rethinking Faculty Roles and Rewards." *American Behavioral Scientist, 41*(5): 604–754.

Tierney, William G., ed. (1999). *Faculty Productivity: Facts, Fictions, and Issues.* New York: Falmer Press.

Trower, Cathy A. (1996). *Tenure Snapshot.* New Pathways Working Paper Series, Inquiry #2. Washington, D.C.: American Association for Higher Education.

Literature on Organizational Change

Baldridge, J. Victor, and Terrence E. Deal. (1975). *Managing Change in Educational Organizations.* Berkeley, CA: McCutchan.

Birnbaum, Robert. (1988). *How Colleges Work: The Cybernetics of Academic Organization and Leadership.* San Francisco: Jossey-Bass.

Bolman, Lee G., and Terrence E. Deal. (1991). *Reframing Organizations.* San Francisco: Jossey-Bass.

Cohen, Michael D., and James G. March. (1986). *Leadership and Ambiguity: The American College President.* Boston: Harvard Business School Press.

Eckel, Peter, Barbara Hill, Madeleine Green, and Bill Mallon. (1999). "Reports from the Road: Insights on Institutional Change." *On Change.* Washington, D.C.: American Council on Education.

Heifitz, Ronald A. (1994). *Leadership Without Easy Answers.* Cambridge, MA: The Belknap Press.

Kotter, John P., and Leonard A. Schlesinger. (1979). "Choosing Strategies for Change." *Harvard Business Review, 57*(2): 106–114.

Index